Inclusive Voices in Post-Exilic Judah

Inclusive Voices
in
Post-Exilic Judah

Anna L. Grant-Henderson

A Michael Glazier Book

THE LITURGICAL PRESS
Collegeville, Minnesota

www.litpress.org

Cover design by David Manahan, O.S.B. Illustration: *Isaiah, the Prophet*, fresco detail by Raphael, 1511–1512, Church of Sant' Agostino, Rome. (Quotation: Isaiah 26:2-3a).

1   2   3   4   5   6   7   8

Library of Congress Cataloging-in-Publication Data

Grant-Henderson, Anna L., 1941–
    Inclusive voices in post-exilic Judah / Anna L. Grant-Henderson.
        p. cm.
    "A Michael Glazier book."
    Includes bibliographical references and index.
    ISBN 0-8146-5387-1 (alk. paper)
        1. Bible. O.T.—Criticism, interpretation, etc.   2. Covenants—
Biblical teaching.   3. Universalism—Biblical teaching.   I. Title.

BS1199.C6 G72 2002
221.6—dc21

                                                            2001038823

For Jean Pattison Carter (1918–1991)
and
John Smith Lamb Henderson (1914–1978)

Contents

Acknowledgments

I wish to acknowledge the support of Parkin-Wesley College Council for their support and financial help through study leave which enabled this book to be written. Special thanks go to Rev. Dr. Charles Biggs, reader, critic, mentor and friend; Rev. Dr. Laurie Mickan who read and edited and Val Canty who constantly corrects my bibliographies. I am especially privileged to work with colleagues who both care and encourage me, and many students past and present who have contributed in ways they will never know to the final edition of this book.

Abstract

The book demonstrates that there are inclusive voices in the Hebrew Scriptures. These voices became lost as the strong exclusive voices of Ezra/Nehemiah and Ezekiel became dominant. It wasn't until the advent of Christ that inclusive voices again had a part to play, but even then the inclusivity was limited; for example, women and slaves were not accepted into the worshiping communities with equal rights. We need to hear again what the Hebrew Scriptures say to us and be challenged to reflect and act in cases in which we are excluding people by virtue of old prejudices or inappropriate laws.

Inclusivity has responsibilities as well as privileges which the churches need to acknowledge openly and not claim an unreserved inclusivity. Every community sets some boundaries. On the other hand, those who want to be included need to realize there are obligations when one is accepted into a community, and it is not freedom without responsibility.

Because the writings were not able to claim the authority of the Torah, they had to be written claiming a different authority, which in the case of the Hebrew Scriptures was the "righteousness" of God. Not only did they claim this, but their writings were constructed with extraordinary literary skill to confront the authorities of the day. We need to base any assertion for inclusivity on the righteousness of God as well as use literary and communication skills to confront those who still exclude people on the basis of gender, race, physical, or mental differences.

The book demonstrates that many texts which in the past have been named as "universalistic" are nationalistic (Isaiah 40–55) and indeed fail to make clear the the status of the people to whom the proclamation is addressed. The monograph affirms the universalism of God; however, the response to that universalism of God is limited by humans.

Abbreviations

AB	Anchor Bible
ABR	*Australian Biblical Review*
AbrN	*Abr-Nahran*
AnBib	Analecta Biblica
ANVAO	*Avhandlinger utgitt av Det Norske Videnskaps-Akademi I Oslo*
ASTI	*Annual of the Swedish Theological Institute*
BDB	F. Brown, S. R. Driver, and C. A. Briggs, *A Hebrew and English Lexicon of the Old Testament*, Oxford, 1907
BHS	*Biblica Hebraica Stuttgartensia*
Bibl	*Biblica*
BJRL	*Bulletin of the John Rylands Library*
BN	*Biblische Notizen*
BR	*Biblical Research*
BTB	*Biblical Theological Bulletin*
BWANT	Beiträge zur wissenschaft vom Alten und Neuen Testament
BZ	*Biblische Zeitschrift*
BZAW	Beihefte zur *Zeitschrift für die alttestamentliche Wissenschaft*
BZNF	Biblische Zeitschrift, Neue Folge
CBC	Cambridge Bible Commentary
CBQ	*Catholic Biblical Quarterly*
CR:BS	*Currents in Research: Biblical Studies*
CUP	Cambridge University Press
EvTh	*Evangelische Theologie*
ExpT	*Expository Times*
FOTL	Forms of Old Testament Literature
HBT	*Horizons in Biblical Theology*
HSM	Harvard Semetic Monographs
HTR	*Harvard Theological Review*
HUCA	*Hebrew Union College Annual*
IB	*Interpreter's Bible*
ICC	International Critical Commentary

IDB	Interpreter's Dictionary of the Bible
IQIsa	I Qumran Isaiah Scroll
Int	*Interpretation*
ISBE	International Standard Bible Edition
ITC	International Theological Commentary
ITQ	*Irish Theological Quarterly*
JBL	*Journal of Biblical Literature*
JQR	*Jewish Quarterly Review*
JSNTS	Journal for the Study of the New Testament, Supplement Series
JSOT	*Journal for the Study of the Old Testament*
JSOTS	Journal for the Study of Old Testament, Supplement Series
JSS	*Journal of Semetic Studies*
JThS	*Journal of Theological Studies*
LXX	Greek Translation of the Old Testament (Septuagint)
MT	Masoretic Text
NCB	New Century Bible
NEB	*New English Bible*
NICOT	The New International Commentary on the Old Testament
NIV	New International Version
NRSV	New Revised Standard Version of the Bible
OBT	Overtures in Biblical Theology
OTA	Old Testament Abstracts
OTG	Old Testament Guides
OTL	Old Testament Library
PIBS	*Proceedings of the Irish Bible Society*
RB	*Revue Biblique*
RSV	Revised Standard Version
SBL	*Society for Biblical Literature*
SBT	Studies in Biblical Theology
Sem	*Semeia*
SJT	*Scottish Journal of Theology*
SVT	Supplements to *Vetus Testamentum*
TB	*Tyndale Bulletin*
ThB	Theologische Bücherei
ThZ	*Theologische Zeitschrift*
TLZ	*Theologische Literaturzeitung*
Trans	Translation
TRTR	*The Reformed Theological Review*
UF	*Ugaritic-Forschungen*
UG	*Ugaritic*
UUA	Uppsala Universitets Arsskrift

VT	*Vetus Testamentum*
VTSuppl	Vetus Testamentum Supplement Series
WBC	Word Bible Commentary
ZAW	*Zeitschrift für die alttestamentliche Wissenschaft*

Introduction

To explore the Scriptures is an exciting activity because of the diversity of opinions, experiences, and literary genres that are contained within their pages. The formation of the Bible, especially the Hebrew Scriptures, took many hundreds of years before the present text became fixed as canon.[1] As the writers created their books, they were expressing the revelation and experience of YHWH for their time and situation. It is hardly surprising that we have such diversity and even contradictory messages within the Hebrew Scriptures.

How did the Israelites resolve the tension between such diverse messages within the pages of the Scriptures that are claimed to be authoritative? For example, the Law in Deuteronomy 23:3-6 makes it very clear that Moabites are to be excluded from Israelite society, yet in the story of Ruth, not only do

[1] We have used the term Hebrew Scriptures but, out of respect for the people that use the Hebrew Scriptures as their sacred story, we acknowledge that the Christian Scriptures are arranged differently and many of the Christian Bibles include the Apocrypha that is absent from the Hebrew Scriptures. The particular organization of the books in the Hebrew Scriptures is arranged to make a theological point. For example, Chronicles is the last book because it ends with the Israelite people as exiles in Babylon being charged to go up to Jerusalem. This becomes a living hope to the Jews who lived in exile for nearly one thousand years. The last book in the Christian arrangement of the Hebrew Scriptures is the twelfth book of the minor prophets, Malachi. This follows the arrangement that gathers together the forms of literature and ends with the prophetic books that point forward to Christ. When we look at the book of Ruth, we find that it is placed differently in each canon. In the Hebrew Scriptures, Ruth is a part of the Writings or Kethubim, while in the Christian version of the Hebrew Scriptures, Ruth comes between Judges and 1 Samuel (the Former Prophets).

Mahlon and Chilion marry Moabite wives but Ruth is accepted into the Israelite community, which is in direct contradiction to the Torah (Genesis–Deuteronomy). When the Scriptures were finalized, they were not made into one consistent message, but the diverse experiences and understanding of YHWH were all left within their pages.[2] It is likely a modern editor would have screened out the contradictions and made the messages compatible. Thankfully this was not the case, and we have the richness and diversity of multiple views to explore in our study of the Bible.

Our task in this monograph will be to explore the diverse and even contradictory messages about foreigners (נכר). We are omitting any discussion of the Oracles against the nations, which are dealt with in other monographs. Instead, we shall concentrate on passages/books that refer to the acceptance of foreigners within the worshiping community of Israel (Isa 56–66, Ruth). We shall include texts that speak in some sense of an acceptance of foreigners, but which may not be explicit about the status of the foreigner within the Israelite community. We have chosen to take as a priority those texts that use the Hebrew root נכר, mainly because it is used in post-exilic literature and clearly refers to those people who come from a land other than Israel. When נכר is used, the writer is intending something different from a sojourner (גור)—one who has come and settled in the land either temporarily or permanently.

We use the term "inclusive voices" to refer to a particular attitude that is found in some of the passages. This attitude can be present in an overt way, as in Isaiah 56–66 in which the writer depicts the foreigners asserting their right to be included within the Israelite community. On the other hand, the attitude may be depicted more subtly by the writer telling a story in which the foreigner becomes part of the Israelite community, as recounted in the book of Ruth.

It is evident in the study of the Bible that many different attitudes, ideas, and thoughts are present in the Scriptures and to suggest that there is a unity in thought is simply erroneous. The

---

[2] In later Midrashic writings such as Ruth Rabbah, the commentary validates the acceptance of Ruth into the community.

Bible supports ethnic cleansing (Deut 12:2) and slavery (Lev 25:6) and at the same time declares that everyone who joins themselves to the Lord is acceptable in the house of prayer (Isa 56:6-7). Texts can support many agendas, and it is well to recognize the diversity and ambiguity of the biblical messages before we claim any moral high position, based on the authority of the Bible.

We shall examine texts and books in the Hebrew Scriptures that appear to support the claim that people other than Israelites are acceptable within the worshiping community. To this end the books of Ruth and Jonah, Isaiah 56–66 and other selected texts (Isaiah 19, 1 Kgs 8:44) will be examined as examples of inclusive voices. In recent years feminist writers have raised awareness of women's voices that are present in the Scriptures. When we discuss the implications for our study, we want them to be significant for any group that may be marginalized and excluded by the Church on the grounds of: color, sexual preference, gender, age, physical or mental ability (chapter 6 offers some insights which have arisen from this study).

Although we have chosen to use the term "inclusive voices" rather than stay with an older term "universalism," there is still the necessity to explore how universalism has been understood within the biblical context in past scholarly writings. After a brief look at the term universalism, we give a definition that underpins our study and the term "inclusive voices."

"Universalism" in its broadest sense designates the view that all creatures will be saved. The theological implications of this interpretation have been debated by theologians through the centuries. Origen drew on the view from Justinian (543 C.E.) that there would be a final restoration of all things, after a temporary punishment for the devils and the wicked.[3] The opponents of universalism believed this view failed to take seriously moral evil and sin. In the twentieth century Karl Barth and K. Rahner have universalistic tendencies in their writings, which come close to the definition above.[4]

---

[3] G. Wainwright, "Universalism," 1049.

[4] J. Hastings, *Encyclopaedia of Religion and Ethics*, vol. 12, 529–35. S. Neill, G. Anderson, J. Goodwin, eds., *Concise Dictionary of the Christian World Mission*, 628.

In the study of the Hebrew Scriptures "universalism" has been perceived as present in its broad definition. However, many scholars failed to discern any significant difference between the various forms of universalism portrayed in the Hebrew Scriptures.

The *Oxford Dictionary of the Christian Church* acknowledges a more limited view of universalism which is present in the Hebrew Scriptures: "The anti-nationalism teaching of certain of the later Hebrew prophets (Deutero-Isaiah, Jonah) are that God's purposes covered not only the Jewish race but also at least some men [sic] of other nations."[5] Allen in his commentary on Jonah makes an interesting separation in meaning:

> Universalism is an ambiguous term: it may denote the universal power and concern of Yahweh, as Amos construed it (cf. Amos 9:7); or it may mean something quite different, such as the personal self-revelation and grace of Yahweh, who throws open to Gentiles the covenant relationship that hitherto was Israel's privilege.[6]

The sense that God is a universalistic God is portrayed from the very first chapter of Genesis, in which God is the creator of heaven and earth. In the next eleven chapters of Genesis, humanity is spoken of in a generic sense and the Hebrew Scriptures only become particular about the relationship between Israel and YHWH with the commands and promises to Abraham in Genesis 12. In the pre-exilic literature the nations are often depicted as under the control of God, and they are used by God for his purposes to punish Israel and Judah. In the post-exilic literature, God uses the Persians to bring release for the exiles and in other texts the nations are still the enemies of Israel. On the other hand, in the book of Jonah, God's universal care is described in the way that the repentance of Nineveh is acceptable to God (Jon 4:11). There is very little dispute among scholars that God's nature is universalistic in the Hebrew Scriptures.

[5] F. L. Cross and E. A. Livingstone, eds., *The Oxford Dictionary of the Christian Church*, 1415.

[6] L. C. Allen, *The Books of Joel, Obadiah, Jonah and Micah*, 190.

The second half of Allen's definition is the one on which scholars have diverse views. Although Allen fails to give an example of his second definition, both Ruth and Isaiah 56–66 fall into this category.

One has to study closely the texts of the Hebrew Scriptures to appreciate the variations of this theological ideal that believes that all people are to be included within the saving purposes of God. It is inappropriate to impose an interpretation that embodies only a broad interpretation of universalism on all the texts and fails to recognize the limited views of universalism that are present in others.

As we explore the various forms of "universalism/inclusive voices" in the Hebrew Scriptures, we find that what could at first be perceived as universalism is an elevated view of nationalism. Indeed, in some instances the universalism is not for the benefit of the person, but in order to bring greater glory to YHWH. In our study of the texts we ought to hear what the text is saying rather than impose any presuppositions about universalism onto it.

In the 1940s and 1950s scholars such as S. Blank, S. Mowinckel, and H. H. Rowley believed the pinnacle of missionary activity and outreach was represented in the theology of Isaiah 40–55.[7] The servant will reach out to all peoples of the earth and offer them the way to salvation.[8] The assumptions behind these studies were that the nations outside Israel would be accepted as equal and they would be able to share fully in the worship and privileges of belonging to the Yahwistic faith.

This view of salvation began to be questioned in the 1980s and 1990s by a number of scholars. Their suggestions are reviewed in chapter 3, when we look specifically at the texts which have been proposed as universalistic in Isaiah 40–55. We need to do this exercise in order to see the difference between the theology that is present in Isaiah 40–55 and the theology in the texts we shall explore from Isaiah 56–66, Jonah, and Ruth. This monograph does not argue for a linear development of an

---

[7] S. Blank, *Prophetic Faith in Israel*. S. Mowinckel, *He That Cometh*, trans., G. W. Anderson. H. H. Rowley, *Israel's Mission to the World*.

[8] Mowinckel, 207.

understanding of "universalism/inclusive voices," but it attempts to demonstrate the variety of understandings present in the Hebrew Scriptures.

The working definition of "inclusive voices" for this monograph is that the offer of salvation is to all people, who if they choose to respond will receive the same benefits and responsibilites as the Israelites and who will be included in the worshiping community. We note at this point that we shall be pursuing the issue of universalism as it applies to humans. However, the view of God as universalistic is not under discussion in this monograph.

Any offer of salvation by God seeks a response from people by virtue of the fact that God's unconditional offer of grace contains some expectations, such as—"love the Lord your God only, hold fast to the covenant and be obedient." This could be perceived as exclusive in that people can only belong to a worshiping community if there is a response which includes within it certain expectations. In that sense it is exclusive, but the initial offer of salvation should be inclusive of everyone and without conditions, prior to a person's turning to God and acceptance of the offer. We raise this issue here because it needs to be thought through carefully. It covers major theological issues. Thus, if we extend the statement we made about God expecting certain behavioral responses, does this mean that grace is conditional? For example, people who join a Yahwistic or Christian community have to abide by basic covenantal requirements and, therefore, unconditional acceptance ceases to continue once a person wants to belong to a worshiping community. In the Uniting Church in Australia members are expected to be baptized, and if this requirement is not met the person cannot become a voting member or elder in a congregation. Therefore, we want to say that grace is unconditional. However, human institutions set requirements once a person has confessed Christ as Lord and wants to become a full member of a worshiping community. People who make claims to belong to certain communites need to realize there are responsibilities and privileges in belonging.

Chapters 1, 2, and 4 concentrate on those passages (Isa 56–66, Ruth, Jonah, and certain other Scriptures) that are perceived to come closest to the understanding of inclusive voices given above. However, we know that this view of inclusivism failed to become the dominant voice in the Scriptures and the voice of exclusion became the norm until the time of Christ. The post-exilic Scriptures that depict this voice of exclusion are particularly evident in Ezra/Nehemiah and Ezekiel. The different views that are present may represent not only conflicting voices but also the voices of particular groups within the community. These issues are explored in chapter 5.

Our final chapter explores how such a radical inclusiveness, that is present in some texts of the Hebrew Scriptures, has been able to remain within the canon of the Scriptures. We show how some of these voices have been used in the Gospels to support a message that is intended for all people. Furthermore, how does this affect our communities today if we recognize and give due weight to these Scriptures? The discussion takes in an article by G. J. Wenham, "The Gap between Law and Ethics in the Bible."[9] He suggests we have misinterpreted stories in the Old Testament because of our failure to understand the ethical principle that governs the lives of the people of the time. Furthermore, he suggests that this ethical stance is not always the same as the Law and, indeed, "ethics is much more than keeping the law."[10] In "biblical terms righteousness involves more than living by the decalogue and the other laws in the Pentateuch."[11] It is this last point that has direct application both to the proclamation in Isaiah 56–66, and to present-day situations, in which the "law" is used to exclude people from full acceptance in our church communities. To use ethical principles in application of the Scriptures is congruent with the overall purpose of God, who wants the best for all living creatures. We propose from our study that God and Christ chose to work from a base of righteousness, justice, and love, and this should be the governing tenet by which we live within community.

[9] G. J. Wenham, "The Gap between Law and Ethics in the Bible," 17–29.
[10] Ibid., 18.
[11] Ibid., 19.

1

•••••●•●•••••

Isaiah 56:1-8

Isaiah 56:1-8 played a crucial role in discovering the insights which form the basis of this monograph. In these verses the foreigner and the eunuch are acceptable in the house of the Lord despite the explicit laws of exclusion in the Torah. Therefore, they have to make a claim for inclusion based on the ethical principle of righteousness and justice. The particular Hebrew word נכר used for "foreigner" makes connections to other parts of the Hebrew Scriptures and challenges the reader to consider how this word is used to confront the Israelite community. In order to make these claims we shall deal with the exegetical issues in detail. Furthermore, we propose that these verses are the prologue to the remaining eleven chapters, Isaiah 56:9–66:24 and, indeed, we argue that Isaiah 56–66 is created as a unity with the express purpose of advocating the inclusion of foreigners over and against the proclamations of Ezra/Nehemiah and Ezekiel. However, Isaiah 56:1-8 makes it clear that inclusion brings with it responsibilities as well as privileges.

For the last hundred years Isaiah 56:1-8 has been regarded, with a few exceptions, as the opening verses of a discrete body of literature designated as Trito-Isaiah or Third Isaiah (56–66).[1] The passages at either end of chapters 56–66, Isaiah 56:1-8 and

---

[1] W.A.M. Beuken, "The Main Themes of Trito-Isaiah," 67–87. J. Blenkinsopp, "Second Isaiah—Prophet of Universalism," 83–103. P. D. Hanson, *The Dawn of Apocalyptic*, 389.

66:18-24, are referred to often as "bookends,"[2] which most scholars suggest are later additions.[3] A major question is: were the bookends added at a much later time as most scholars believe, or were the chapters deliberately structured at the one time, using material from different sources and historical periods? This monograph has chosen after due research to work on the basis that Isaiah 56–66 was created as a unit. A table in the Appendix (table I) gives a summary of those scholars who argue that Isaiah 56–66 had one or more redactions in its growth to the final form. There is little consistency by scholars on which chapters and passages come from which period, and it becomes a pointless exercise to pursue. We shall point out some problems associated with the proposed idea that 56:1-8 and 66:18-24 are bookends and suggest a new proposition for these passages.

Isaiah 56:1-8 is not only very different in theological content from Isaiah 1–55, but its theology is unique in the Hebrew Scriptures.[4] The offer of salvation is extended now to both eunuchs (v. 4) and foreigners (v. 6) who accept the covenant and who will be treated as equal to the Israelites themselves (v. 7). This seems to contradict the law in Deuteronomy 23:1-8, which says that no eunuch, bastard, Ammonite, or Moabite shall enter the assembly of the Lord. Ezekiel 44:4-14 holds a strong polemic against foreigners entering into the Temple and in

---

[2] K. Koenen, *Ethik und Eschatologie im Tritojesajabuch*, 212. K. Pauritsch, *Die Neue Gemeinde*, 46–48. H. Odeberg, *Trito-Isaiah, (Isaiah lvi–lxvi). A Literary and Linguistic Analysis*, 27. G. J. Polan, *In the Ways of Justice Toward Salvation: A Rhetorical Analysis of Isaiah 56–59*, 324. C. Westermann, *Isaiah 40–66*, 305.

[3] Blenkinsopp, "Second Isaiah—Prophet of Universalism," 97. Hanson, *The Dawn of Apocalyptic*, 388. D. R. Jones, *Isaiah 56–66 and Joel*, 20. Pauritsch, *Die Neue Gemeinde*, 46. Polan, *In the Ways of Justice Towards Salvation*, 18–24. J. J. Scullion, "Studies in Isaiah cc. 56–66," 156. J. D. Smart, *History and Theology in Second Isaiah*, 230. Westermann, *Isaiah 40–66*, "Practically all editors, even those who—as, for example, Kessler—regard Isaiah 56–66 as a unity, look on the opening and the closing verses (Isa 56:1-8 and 66:18-24) as later additions," 305.

[4] H. Donner, "Jesaja LVI 1-7: Ein Abrogationsfall Innerhalb des Kanons—Implikationen und Konsequenzen," 98.

Isaiah 60–62 foreigners are to be subservient to the Israelites and not equal, as suggested in Isaiah 56:1-8.

As we consider the structure of Isaiah 56:1-8, it becomes clear that the literary skill employed is quite remarkable, and we shall point out how language and structure enhance the theology.

As we noted above, the claim by Trito-Isaiah was in opposition to the Torah, and so the very first clause makes the claim that the message to follow comes from God. "Thus says the Lord" (v. 1), known as a message formula, gives the following proclamation an authority beyond that of the writer.[5] The Lord has said it, and so it must be heard as God speaking through this prophet. Westermann disagrees that the use of the formula makes the material which follows an authentic word of God to the prophet. Instead he describes Isaiah 56:3-8 as "regulations," on which the writer is attempting to confer the authority of the prophetic word.[6] We agree with Westermann when he says that the writer wants to have the authoritative word of God for his writings, but disagree that it is simply regulations. Furthermore, Trito-Isaiah has a different message to that of Deutero-Isaiah, and his purpose in writing is not that of preserving the ideas of Deutero-Isaiah. Westermann believes that Deutero-Isaiah embodies the highest theological proclamation of salvation in the Hebrew Scriptures, which impedes his ability to discern the creativity and literary skill of Trito-Isaiah.

Recognizing literary changes is important. A particular form must not be imposed on every written piece of material. The writers of the Hebrew Scriptures were both creative and free to change forms and concepts if it suited their theological purpose. Therefore, it is essentially a question of observing the new theological emphases wrought by the literary changes. In the case of Isaiah 56:1, we believe it is the author's purpose to gain authoritative status for the following proclamation in 56:2-8.

No identity is given to the people addressed by the exhortation in verse 1a. However, verse 1a uses two imperatives to stress the action that God requires of the people, on the assumption

---

[5] Pauritsch, *Die Neue Gemeinde,* 49. "The message formula authorizes the entire work as the message of God."

[6] Westermann, *Isaiah 40–66,* 305.

by the speaker that the people have returned from exile and are ready to carry out these injunctions.[7] This is different from the previous prophetic speeches in which the warning speech was often the foundation for the offer of "return" to the exiles.[8] Here, the injunction is to "keep justice and do righteousness," for the people do not have to wait long for God's salvation to be revealed.[9] The imperatives encourage the people to act rightly while waiting for God's revelation.

We suggest that the literary structure (vv. 1-2) and the combination of the two important theological concepts משפט and צדק (justice and righteousness) serve as the principle for the new and unprecedented inclusion of those people spoken of in verses 3-8 who were normally excluded by the Law. In verse 1a the people are expected to act in the same way as God acts towards them, with the encouragement that God's salvation and righteousness is near (v. 1b). The two imperatives used in verse 1a do not pick up the sense of the conditional requirements of pre-exilic writers.[10] Nor can קרוב (near) be seen to be conditional. The use of two infinitives ("come" and "reveal") with

---

[7] References in 56:7 to "a house of prayer" which is on the "holy mountain" suggest that they are back in Jerusalem and not in Babylon where there are no references ever to worshiping on the holy mountain in a house of prayer.

[8] Pauritsch, *Die Neue Gemeinde*, suggests the writer in 56:1b has assumed that the hearers have already "returned," 41.

[9] Isaiah 51–52 proclaims the salvation of God for the exiles together with their return to Jerusalem. The material in Isaiah 56 addresses those who have returned to Jerusalem. If they have returned, why is salvation still to come? R. P. Carroll, in his *When Prophecy Failed: Reactions and Responses to Failure in the Old Testament Prophetic Traditions*, suggests that is because the promised Temple and peace that was prophesied have not yet come to fruition. The writer has to rationalize and give further hope. This occurs with the exhortation and promise of the salvation still to come, 152–54.

[10] G. Emmerson, *Isaiah 56–66*, states, "the right action (justice and righteousness) to which society is summoned is regarded not as the means of securing God's saving intervention, but, on the contrary, as the appropriate preparation of the community which is necessary because YHWH's deliverance is imminent," 100.

"lamhed" prefixes, usually translated "to come and to reveal" are translated here as participles. It is an unusual construction, reinforcing the movement in theological thought that has shifted from the proclamation of God's salvation in Jerusalem (Isa 46:13) to the need for the people to behave appropriately (Isa 56:1). Salvation will come and it is close at hand. It is not dependent on the people doing justice nor is it a response to salvation. The writer wants to encourage the people to behave in the right way while still affirming the promise of Deutero-Isaiah (46:13). The application of this form of the verb (will come, will be revealed) leaves no doubt that it will happen. In this sense it corresponds to many announcements in Deutero-Isaiah about how God will act, but the difference is the (non-conditional) injunction in verse 1b, which makes the structure unique to the writer of Isaiah 56–66.

A development of this idea is demonstrated by Blenkinsopp. He understands verse 1 as a commentary on Isaiah 46:13 and 51:5, which takes the message further by associating it with both ethical and eschatological issues.[11] The contexts in Deutero-Isaiah refer to Zion (46:13) and the commandment to hear and listen (51:4, 7). The association with the preceding contexts reinforces the suggestion above, that it is a deliberate structure to lead into the radical proclamation of verses 3-8.[12]

In view of this discussion the appropriate translation of צדקתי in verse 1b is "my righteousness." The repetition of the word for righteousness appears deliberate, and we see no reason to follow the English translations of "my deliverance." The use of righteousness as the parallel to "my salvation" makes the theological point that righteousness is part of salvation. This structure is crucial in understanding and interpreting the following verses.

---

[11] Blenkinsopp, "Second Isaiah—Prophet of Universalism," 95.

[12] J. Bastiaens and others, *Trito-Isaiah. An exhaustive Concordance of Isa. 56–66, especially with reference to Deutero-Isaiah. An example of computer assisted research,* 5. This study demonstrates that Trito-Isaiah is not dependent on Deutero-Isaiah when the former uses the term "righteousness." Each time we have to determine its meaning in the new context and the continuity with Deutero-Isaiah only plays a discrete part, unless Trito-Isaiah clearly takes over a text from Deutero-Isaiah.

Righteousness in the Hebrew Scriptures is more than the Law. The Law is the minimum requirement, but righteousness is more than keeping the Law.[13] Israel is in relationship with God and made in God's image. This relationship calls for people to live in love which is more than simply obedience to the Law. Consequently, in the context of Isaiah 56:1-8 salvation includes the need for righteousness and those who keep this will be blessed. Furthermore, this righteousness includes the acceptance of foreigners and eunuchs who are loyal and committed to the Lord. The writer is calling on the relationship ideal of the covenant in order to counter the claims made by Ezra/Nehemiah and Ezekiel who call on the Law for their policies of exclusion. We cannot emphasize too highly the critical role of verse 1 in setting the theological boundaries for interpreting the remainder of this section and indeed Isaiah 56–66 as a whole. Israel knows from experience that God acts justly and therefore the commands in verse 1 model God's behavior towards them which they are expected now to model towards others (v. 2).

This is a new and developed concept by the writer of chapters 56–66 that has been demonstrated in verse 1. Moreover, the author has brought together the two emphases of the people's relationship with God previously presented separately in the earlier chapters of Isaiah. First, in Isaiah 1–39 the emphasis is on the people's behavior as required by God in order to avoid punishment (Isa 1:16-20, 28:16-22). Second, in Isaiah 40–55 the first-person promises of God are not dependent on the people's actions but assume that the people will follow and do what God requires (41:10; 42:1, 6-9, 14-16, 43:2ff., 44:22).

Trito-Isaiah has brought together both the requirements demanded of people (56:1a) and the unconditional promise of Deutero-Isaiah (56:1b) within the one verse.[14] Salvation (1b) is not dependent on whether the people have kept justice and righteousness, but on the promise implied in the words "for

---

[13] G. J. Wenham, "The Gap between Law and Ethics in the Bible," 19.

[14] R. Rendtorff, "Zur Komposition des Buches Jesaja," 295–320, names the use of צדק/משפט in Isaiah 1–39 as human righteousness and in Isaiah 40–55 in which צדק is associated with שוע, as divine salvation. He supports our claim that the two emphases are brought together in Isaiah 56:1.

soon." The people are encouraged to continue waiting for God's salvation. Further, they are exhorted to make a response, but if they do not "keep justice and do righteousness" there is no threatened withdrawal of God's salvation. Salvation is coming, and requires people to act ethically, but it is an exhortation and not a condition. Isaiah 56:1 demonstrates this unique association of exhortation and promise in the proclamation about the relationship with God.[15]

Many scholars place verses 1 and 2 together.[16] They agree that these verses were originally separate but have been deliberately connected as part of the construction of Isaiah 56:1-8. The purpose of verse 2 is to act as the hinge verse for the passage and to make explicit the general injunctions of verse 1. One argument against this suggestion is based on the possibility that verse 2 belongs to the Wisdom genre; therefore, it cannot be a continuation of verse 1b because that is the word of God.[17] Our examination of the structure of verses 1-8 confirms that verse 2 acts as a link: "this" (זאת) and "in it" (בה) in verse 2a refer back to the general directive in verse 1a which points us forward to the specific action in verse 2b. The evidence points to a deliberate structure and theological intent in the way verse 2 has been placed in its pivotal position.

[15] R. Rendtorff, "Isaiah 56:1 as a Key to the Formation of the Book of Isaiah," says that the combination of God's righteousness with God's salvation is present for the first time in Isaiah thereby emphasizing that something new is intended, 183. Rendtorff also points out that the imperatives in 56:1a are used for the first time in Isaiah. Because of these linguistic usages, he believes that Isaiah 56:1 is both a turning point in theological message and also continuous with Isaiah 1–39, 40–55, 185.

[16] Pauritsch, *Die Neue Gemeinde,* 31. Scullion, "Studies in Isaiah cc. 56–66," 94. Snaith, "Isaiah 40–66," 222. R. N. Whybray, *Isaiah 40–66,* 196.

[17] Pauritsch, *Die Neue Gemeinde,* 31, 32, 35. Pauritsch notes that a number of scholars attest that verse 2 is wisdom in origin and content; compare Psalms 1, 15, 106:3, Job. E. Sehmsdorf, "Studien zur Redaktionsgeschichte von Jesaja 56–66," is not wanting to argue for a new beginning or separation from verse 1. He agrees with the wisdom connection and cites further passages to those above, Psalm 119:1f.; 1 Kings 10:8; 2 Chronicles 9:7; Daniel 12:12. Comparable passages are Job 35:8; 2 Samuel 7:14; Jeremiah 32:19; compare Isaiah 49:18, 31; 50:40; 51:43.

"Man" (אנוש) and "son of man" (בן-אדם) can be interpreted as referring to the Israelites alone. However, in the context of the verses that follow, the evidence points to the inclusion also of the foreigner and eunuch. Verse 4a declares that the eunuchs who keep the Sabbath will receive a number of stated blessings (v. 5).[18] In verse 6b the terms become open to everyone, which leads into the high point of the passage (v. 7).

Verse 2b reveals an association with both the ethical requirements (vv. 1a, 2a) and the Sabbath commandment (v. 2b). The association is present also in Ezekiel 20:10-24; 22:8, 26. Both Deutero-Isaiah and Ezekiel portray an increased emphasis on the Sabbath commandment[19] and employ the particular word "profane" in the new relationship between the ethical demands and Sabbath commandment. If we were certain about the time of writing of Ezekiel 20, 22 and accepted a close similarity between these texts, it could help us date Isaiah 56:1-8.[20] However, we have dates for the final production of the book of Ezekiel that vary from 590 B.C.E. (Snaith) down into the fourth century (Biggs).[21] This variation makes it difficult to use Ezekiel as a reference point to date Isaiah 56:1-8.

---

[18] Sehmsdorf, "Studien zur Redaktionsgeschicte von Jesaja 56–66," believes the use of the plural here could indicate two possibilities: one, a connection with Ezekiel where the plural is used twelve times and two, a direct reference to the Levitical law as a satirical comment on the law which forbids the admittance of foreign people to the community, 545. Biggs, "Exegesis in the book of Ezekiel," points out in his work the close connection between Ezekiel and the Holiness code.

[19] Scullion, "Studies in Isaiah cc. 56–66," does not see this period as the start of Sabbath observance as it has been part of the ongoing Israelite tradition, 95. He believes M. Noth is right when he says that the importance of the Sabbath increased markedly during the exile, but it was not the start of its observance, 155.

[20] Odeberg, *Trito-Isaiah, (Isaiah lvi–lxvi)*, states, "the dependence of Trito-Isaiah on Ezekiel is upon the redactional form of the book," 29, 38. This still leaves uncertainty about an exact date of the final form of Ezekiel and therefore also Isaiah 56–66.

[21] C. R. Biggs, "The Role of the *nasi* in the Programme for the Restoration in Ezek 40–48," A paper given to the Adelaide Theological Circle, 1988, 16. Held in his possession.

The Sabbath was significant in the life of Israel before the exile, but it took on new and important theological dimensions for the people during and after the exile.[22] Exile was the context in which the Sabbath commandment came to be important as one way of maintaining the relationship with God. This is seen in the laws, especially in Leviticus (23:34, 43), Chronicles (1 Chr 23:31; 2 Chr 8:13, 31:3, 36:21), Nehemiah (9:14; 13:19-22), and the prophetic writings of Jeremiah (17:19-27) as well as Isaiah and Ezekiel. Only Isaiah in the above-mentioned Scriptures includes foreigners in the Sabbath command. The offer to the man (Isa 56:2), eunuch (Isa 56:4), and everyone (Isa 56:6) is unique in the Hebrew Scriptures. Foreigners and eunuchs will be blessed when they keep the Sabbath: a requirement that is part of the privilege of belonging. Trito-Isaiah has used the Sabbath command for his own purposes. We are challenged to see the way words or phrases that are used in one context can confront old ideas when employed in a new setting.

Verses 3-8 present in detail two categories of people who will be blessed when they keep the Sabbath and do no evil. The un-expected factor is the identity of the two groups of people—eunuchs and foreigners. Consequently we appear to have a passage whose inclusive proclamation surpasses any preceding proclamation of universalism in the Hebrew Scriptures and is contrary to the Law in a number of places.

Certain Hebrew words describe different categories of foreigner. First, we examine נכר (foreigner), which is used in Isaiah 56:3, 6. According to listings in BDB and Clines it occurs mainly in post-exilic writings.[23] In Isaiah 56–66, נכר (foreigner) is employed in two very different theological contexts. Isaiah 56:1-8 and 66:18-24 includes foreigners as equals and Isaiah 60–62 portrays foreigners as subservient to the Israelites. The employment of נכר (foreigner) in Isaiah 56:1-8 appears to be an

---

[22] Odeberg, *Trito-Isaiah, (Isaiah lvi–lxvi)*, 18. H. McKay, "From Evidence to Edifice: Four Fallacies about the Sabbath," disputes the idea that the Sabbath became a holy day in Israel prior to the last two centuries B.C.E., 179–99.

[23] F. Brown, S. R. Driver and C. A. Briggs, *The New Brown-Driver-Briggs*, 648.

example of how this writer takes words and gives them a contrary sense from their normal application. We have named this literary technique as an oxymoron because its use intends to startle and to challenge the readers to rethink their attitude to foreigners.

Other words in the Hebrew Scriptures to denote stranger, foreigner, or sojourner are גור (sojourner), מגור (a temporary lodging). Both are derived from the root גור[24] and except for a few cases the verb גור is translated "to sojourn" (fifty-four times).[25] These words are used frequently in the Hebrew Scriptures, especially in the Pentateuch, but they are also scattered throughout the other books. When תושב (alien) is employed either in the singular or plural, according to BDB, it is late and found solely in P writings, denoting in Genesis, Exodus, Leviticus, and Numbers, a resident of a more temporary kind than the גור (sojourner), Lev 22:10.[26]

Another word employed for stranger is צור (to turn aside), especially for lodging, with its derivatives describing a strange thing, place or person, hence foreigner. Again it is scattered throughout the Hebrew Scriptures, but most commonly used in the prophets Isaiah, Jeremiah, Ezekiel, and Hosea.[27]

The writer of Isaiah 56–66 intentionally uses נכר (foreigner) rather than תושב (sojourner) to emphasize that the person belonged to another race or nation and was not simply a temporary sojourner who may or may not be a foreigner. By using this word נכר (foreigner) in a converse manner to other contexts, the writer is making a new and exceptional statement. Where previously the writings (other than in Isa 56:1-8) had excluded the foreigner from the Israelite community, now the foreigner who is from another nation or race may belong to the covenant community of God as an equal with the Israelite people. Orlinsky fails to recognize the enormity of the statement in Isaiah 56:3-8.[28]

---

[24] Ibid., 158a.

[25] Ibid., 157.

[26] Ibid., 444b.

[27] Ibid., 266a, b.

[28] H. M. Orlinsky, "Nationalism-Universalism and Internationalism in Ancient Israel," says "the whole passage, far from articulating interna-

We turn our attention now to the phrase "the foreigner who has joined himself to the Lord." Whybray and Westermann suggest it represents the person known as the proselyte, a technical word not used until New Testament times.[29] Indeed, Whybray believes that Deutero-Isaiah had envisaged and approved such a phenomenon in Isaiah 44:5. Rather, the text speaks solely of Jacob's descendants, and this cannot support his suggestion. Deutero-Isaiah contains no evidence for the acceptance of foreigners into a covenant relationship with the God of the Israelites.

Westermann suggests the phrase "who has joined himself to the Lord" appears with the same meaning in Isaiah 14:1, where it is obviously a current designation for a proselyte. However, the term used is נר and Isaiah 14:2 suggests that after the aliens have joined the Israelites they will become slaves. This could be an example of another oxymoron rather than Isaiah 14:1 acting as a parallel for Isaiah 56:3.

After the foreigner has become joined to the Lord, he is no longer allowed to say that the Lord will separate him from the Israelite people. The cited complaint in verse 3a, which reflects the Torah requirements of Deuteronomy 23:1-8, expresses the previously inapplicable and hopeless situation of the speakers (no eunuch or foreigner shall enter the assembly of the Lord).[30]

---

tionalism, *simply asserts* (my emphasis) that those non-Israelites who adopt and demonstrate their obedience to God's commandments and institutions would be permitted to become members of his covenanted community in the land of Israel," 219. This statement of Orlinsky fails to appreciate the message of Isaiah 56:1-8 in light of the Law and proclamations in Ezekiel, Ezra/Nehemiah.

[29] Whybray, *Isaiah 40–66*, 197. Westermann, *Isaiah 40–66*, ". . . this phrase is obviously a designation for a proselyte current at the time," 312. J. Muilenburg, "Isaiah Chapters 40–66," 503. The LXX translates the Hebrew "ger" as proselyte which may be the reason why some scholars have used the term which did not become a technical term for a convert until New Testament times.

[30] Westermann, *Isaiah 40–66*, quotes Deuteronomy 23:1-8 as the basis for the lament in Isaiah 56:3, 313. S. Sekine, *Die Tritojesajanische Sammlung (Jes 56–66) Redaktionsgeschichtlich Untersucht*, goes so far as to claim that all commentators see verse 3 as dependent on Deuteronomy 23:1-8, 34.

One Jewish scholar, in an attempt to deal with this contradiction to the Torah, points out that a few specific nations are mentioned in Deuteronomy 23:1-8.[31] The Ammonites and the Moabites are specifically refused access to the assembly (Deut 23:3), but children of the third generation of Edomites and Egyptians are allowed into the assembly (Deut 23:7-8).[32] Therefore, Deuteronomy 23:1-8 cannot be taken as a general prohibition against foreigners and in particular Isaiah 56:1-8 is not a contradiction of the Torah. Scullion, Whybray, and Muilenburg acknowledge the specific nations mentioned in the prohibition of Deuteronomy 23:1-8, but they fail to use this as an argument against Westermann's observation (Isa 56:3 reflects Deut 23:1-8).

While Komlash is mainly concerned to demonstrate that there is no contradiction between the Torah and Isaiah 56:1-8, he does raise an important point not generally discussed by other scholars. Is it possible to accept Komlash's observation that the specific nations mentioned in Deuteronomy 23:1-8 are the ones prohibited from the assembly and not every nation as proposed by most commentators? If the prohibition applies to a few, the radical nature of Isaiah 56:1-8 is lessened. Alongside the Deuteronomy passage there are the explicit commands in Ezekiel 44 excluding *all foreigners* from the sanctuary, which indicates that the author/s of Ezekiel 44 interpreted Deuteronomy 23:1-8 to include all foreigners. The Torah command (Deut 23:1-8) may have pertained to a particular historical period, but Ezekiel 44 no longer applied it only to Ammon and Moab in the post-exilic situation.

We turn our attention to another proposal that argues that God is able to reveal new knowledge that is not tied to the authority of the Law.[33] The word of God (Isa 56:1a) is automatically beyond any limitation set by Scripture, even with the authority that the book of Deuteronomy would have gained by the time of the Exile. That break with an old authority is reinforced when portrayed as part of the Eschaton, (v. 1b, "for soon my salvation will come"). Neither the word of God nor his

[31] Y. Komlash, "The Prophecy of Salvation," 11–17.
[32] Ibid.
[33] Donner, "Jesaja LVI 1-7," 85–87.

promise is to be tied to the Law, but rather based on the "new authority" of righteousness. The congregation, unlike the blood-line community of previous generations, will become a confessing congregation based on ethical behavior and Sabbath Holiness. This change in the composition of the congregation will occur before the opening of the Eschaton.

It is YHWH and not the prophet who has replaced the Law with new stipulations: as YHWH revealed the Law to Moses in the past, so now YHWH has the power to bring in new laws. However, Donner not only wants to see it as a corrective to the holy Scripture, but a case of the cancellation of a holy text through the authority of God himself. He admits this is the only place in the Hebrew Scriptures where this occurs, and God alone has the power to abrogate a text.[34]

The idea that Scripture can be annulled is very difficult to apply to the Hebrew Scriptures. This particular text (Isa 56:1-8) continued to be present in the Prophetic Books and was valid for the people of Israel and for Jews. Clearly, God gives new revelations of his purpose and character, but this is added onto the information already given and is not an abrogation of previous knowledge. In summary, God gives new wisdom that does not have to be authorized by either the annulment of the past text or the need to argue that some nations were excluded from the community of YHWH. This possibility of new revelation is important to the writer of Isaiah 56:1-8 if he is to get his message taken seriously as the authoritative word of God. As Zimmerli states, "Prophetic proclamation thus shatters and transforms traditions in order to announce the approach of the Living One."[35]

After examination of the above theories that advance Deuteronomy 23:1-8 as the source of the lament in Isaiah 56:3a and

---

[34] Donner, "Jesaja LVI 1-7," 88. He uses as the basis for his argument an example in the Koran where he demonstrates how a text was canceled by a new revelation, and the earlier one was excluded from having any validity for the people. The case of the Deuteronomic Law is different because it is still both in the Scripture and is still valid for the Jewish people today.

[35] W. Zimmerli, "Prophetic Proclamation and Re-interpretation," 100.

which after examination appear to be flawed, questions are raised about other possible sources. The post-exilic books of Ezra, Nehemiah, and Ezekiel 44 are very condemnatory of foreigners. This aspect, together with the use of the phrase "will surely separate me from his people," may point to the time of Ezra and Nehemiah. If this is the case and in light of the message and demand by Ezra/Nehemiah, it is not surprising that foreigners who had become part of the faith community felt despair. But the writer of Isaiah 56:1-8 uses the negative in verse 3a to deny the demand of Ezra/Nehemiah, assuming that they were written either at the same time or just prior to Isaiah 56:1-8.[36] One can hypothesize that the author took this phrase (the Lord will surely separate me from his people), deliberately inserted it into the text and then denied its message totally by including the following verses (vv. 4-7).[37] The verb בדל (separate) strengthened with the infinitive absolute, "will surely separate me from his people," may be in response to the rigorist measures demanded by Ezra/Nehemiah.[38] Because

---

[36] H.G.M. Williamson, *Ezra, Nehemiah,* posits a two-stage construction of Ezra/Nehemiah, 400 B.C.E. and 300 B.C.E., 46. Ackroyd, *Exile and Restoration,* believes Nehemiah came first and Ezra not until after the turn of the century, 398 B.C.E., 87.

[37] P. C. Beentjes, "Inverted Quotations in the Bible: A Neglected Stylistic Pattern," 506–23. This particular stylistic device has been called Zeidel's Law after an article by M. Zeidel, "Parallels between Isaiah and Psalms," *Sinai* 38, 1955–56. Beentje cites a number of examples in which the actual lines of a quotation have been inverted that calls attention to the content of the quotation, and the reader hears something other than the traditional words, 523. Trito-Isaiah is not using an inverted quotation, but he has the same purpose when he uses "an oxymoron." In Trito-Isaiah the content of the quotation has "converted" the subject of the verb. In this case the foreigners will no longer be separated from the worshiping community of Israel as declared in Ezra/Nehemiah.

[38] Whybray, *Isaiah 40–66,* is happy to support the idea of this passage opposing rigorist measures of the Jews soon after the return to Zion, but not as late as the time of Ezra and Nehemiah, 197. Blenkinsopp, "Second Isaiah—Prophet of Universalism," makes the comment that Isaiah 56:1-8 could be either a response to rigorist measures set in motion or a written record of what is already occurring in the community of faith, 96. Snaith,

there is no consensus on the date of these writings, we could be looking at the end of the fifth century (c. 420–400 B.C.E.) or early fourth century (c. 380 B.C.E.). Therefore, it cannot be used as a definitive argument for dating verses 3-8, but it could be one indicator along with others discerned in this exegesis.

The term "eunuch" is not used in the Law of Deuteronomy 23:1 ("He whose testicles are crushed or whose male member is cut off shall not enter the assembly of the Lord"), but is quoted in relation to this text. "Eunuch" is most probably a foreign word adopted into Jewish culture and found three times in Isaiah, five times in Jeremiah, twice in 2 Kings, and seven times in Daniel 1. Apart from the Kings' references, the remaining texts would be considered exilic or later,[39] which suggests it was a word adopted from their exilic experience and not available before that time.

The understanding from both Deuteronomy 23:1 and Leviticus 21:16-23 leaves us in no doubt that people who have physical "blemishes" are unacceptable in the house of the Lord. Muilenburg suggests that the writer did not know the laws in Deuteronomy or Leviticus and was able to proclaim the acceptance of eunuchs out of ignorance of the Law.[40] His explanation appears unlikely when the writer apparently knew of other laws and writings which he refers to in Trito-Isaiah; for example, the Sabbath law, Deutero-Isaiah (46:13), Psalms (118:5).

"Isaiah 40–66," makes the claim that Chronicles-Ezra-Nehemiah are "really the story of the rise and triumph of the Jewish principle of Habdalah," 224.

[39] Isaiah 39:7, named as exilic by R. E. Clements, *Isaiah 1–39*, 277. For P. R. Ackroyd, "An Interpretation of the Babylonian Exile," 56:3, 4, are post-exilic, 329–35. Jeremiah 29:2; 34:19; 38:7; 41:16; 52:25, all written in prose and named as exilic by E. W. Nicholson, *Preaching to the Exiles*, 122ff., also J. A. Thompson, *The Book of Jeremiah*, 47, note 71. J. Gray, *1 & 11 Kings*, thinks that 2 Kings 9:32 possibly comes from the hand of the Deuteronomic redactor and therefore could be exilic; 2 Kgs 20:18, may have some retouching, 537, 668. R. A. Anderson, *Daniel: Signs and Wonders*, is clear that Daniel 1 was written at the time of the second century B.C.E., xiii. W. S. Towner, *Daniel*, 2.

[40] J. Muilenburg, "Isaiah Chapters 40–66," "the prophet betrays no familiarity with this law," 657.

If the writer did not know the Law, one could propose he was a foreigner himself, not brought up in the Jewish faith and therefore not familiar with the Torah. Scholars have failed to consider this possibility, perhaps because it is so unlikely that even a foreigner could be familiar with some material and not know of the Torah.

A much stronger possibility is the deliberate use of an extreme position by the writer to make a theological case for his proclamation. To use the example of someone who is despised and excluded from the community because of physical disability, but who is presented now as acceptable, is unique in Hebrew Scriptures. The message of 56:1-8 contradicts the Torah and is centuries before its time.[41]

Eunuchs were sexually mutilated men often used for service at the imperial court, especially in harems. Some became prominent at court in other positions, but no eunuch was allowed to enter the Temple. Both Pauritsch and Scullion think that foreigners and eunuchs returned with the Jews from Babylon and sought inclusion within the covenant community, on the basis that this had been the practice in Babylon.[42] However, in light of the adamant refutations by Ezekiel (ch. 44), the Holiness Code (Lev 21:21; 22:10ff.) and later Ezra (10:1ff.) and Nehemiah (13:23ff.), it is hard to envisage that those in exile accepted foreigners and eunuchs into their midst as equals. A further point that would mitigate against the inclusion of eunuchs was the need for those in exile to maintain their own identity. One of the ways this occurred was to exclude anyone who was different

---

[41] Jesus was a living example of someone who confronted expectations. The Jews had an understanding of a Messiah who would be like David. In living out the image of a suffering servant he confronted their expectations. The message in Isaiah 56:1-8 also confronts people's expectations.

[42] Scullion, "Studies in Isaiah cc. 56–66," "Foreigners may well have come to Judah with these Jews who themselves could well have been contaminated with pagan practices. Such is the raw material for the problem of admission of eunuchs and foreigners to the assembly," 157. Pauritsch, *Die Neue Gemeinde*, holds a similar view, 46. We note the tentative suggestions with the "may well" and "could well" for which no evidence is given.

from acceptance into the community. Deutero-Isaiah (44:9-24) and Ezekiel (5:1-12; 20:1-31) demonstrate this facet of exclusivity. It is highly unlikely that foreigners and eunuchs were among those who returned with the exiles to Jerusalem and demanded inclusion into the community.

Verse 3 ends with a negative statement denying the eunuch his right to call himself a "dry tree." The statement by the foreigner in verse 3a is promoted as a technical term for the separation of the Jews from the foreigners. No scholar suggests the same for the eunuch's statement in verse 3b. Nevertheless, the complaint of the eunuch is constructed in the first-person singular to underline the hopelessness of the eunuch's condition. These statements by the foreigner and eunuch are denied in the following verses (vv. 4-7) where the Torah requirements for acceptance into the community are rejected. Verse 3 is a literary structure based around the negative statements "let not . . .," to highlight the theological proclamation.

The message formula, "thus says the Lord" (v. 4a) gives authority for what is to follow and the same arguments hold true here as for verse 1a.

A promise is given to the eunuch (v. 5) that depends on the eunuch keeping the Sabbath, choosing things that please the Lord, and holding fast to the covenant (v. 4). God's promise of salvation and righteousness (56:1) is present, but in order to receive the benefits (v. 5) the eunuchs are required to do these three things (v. 4). The desire by the author of Isaiah 56:1-8 for people to appropriate the promises of God is similar to that of the pre-exilic understanding of covenant. It sounds different from the causative nature of the Mosaic covenant because it uses the verb "to choose." Here, the eunuchs have a choice to receive or not receive the benefits of a relationship with God. This sounds softer, although the consequences may be no different from what is meant in Exodus 19:5: "IF you will obey my voice and keep my commandments, you shall be my own possession among all peoples."

In the Deuteronomic material people have "to turn/repent" (שוב) before God will restore them (30:1-3). This condition is absent in Deutero-Isaiah, where the Lord will restore, lead, guide and save the people (40:1-2). Isaiah 56:1 has both exhortation

(v. 1a) and promise (v. 1b). In Isaiah 56:4-8 the benefits of a relationship with God are listed which include certain requirements (keep the Sabbath, hold fast the covenant). Salvation is offered first, unlike the conditional offers in the Deuteronomic material and pre-exilic prophets. The consequence of the promise is that the people are not held responsible for God's actions: God is free to offer salvation, and people once they respond are expected to honor the relationship by their loyalty to YHWH alone, keeping the covenant and the Sabbath. This understanding is the same for Christians, who, if they choose to accept the grace that is offered freely through Jesus Christ, are then expected to be faithful and follow the ways of Christ. In other words each religious community has expectations of certain behavior from those who commit themselves to its particular ideals: privilege includes responsibility.

In verse 2 there is both a positive and a negative in the Sabbath command: positive—"who keeps the Sabbath," and negative—"not profaning it and who keeps his hand from doing any evil." Verse 4 states these in the positive—"who keep my Sabbaths, who choose things that please me." Repeating the command about the Sabbath indicates its importance to the author and his desire to ensure the readers take account of it. Moreover, the repetition of requirements reinforces the idea that verses 1-8 were deliberately structured with verse 2 as the hinge verse. The extra requirement to "hold fast my covenant" is mentioned both for the eunuchs and the foreigners (v. 6), and this phrase is peculiar to these two verses (vv. 4 and 6).[43] Again, when a command such as this (hold fast my covenant) is repeated, we are charged to realize its significance for Trito-Isaiah.

The promise is specific to the eunuchs because they are not able to have progeny and therefore they are like the "dry tree" in verse 3. They will have a name within the house of the Lord (v. 5) which will be superior to the physical progeny of sons

---

[43] Sekine, *Die Tritojesajanische Sammlung (Jes 56–66)*, is sure that verses 2-6 have a deliberate structure which is detailed with reference to grammar, repeated use of particular phrases (holds fast my covenant) and the naming of both groups in verse 3 with the respective explanations standing chiastically. All point to a deliberate theological intent, 37–38.

and daughters. Further, this promise of "an everlasting name which shall not be cut off" transcends the human condition (v. 5b). God does not punish people because they have been mutilated by other human beings. They are worthy as they are despite any physical blemish. Verse 5b appears to be a pun on the mutilation that occurs when a person is castrated.[44] The literary skill employed in this verse is quite consistent with other aspects of Trito-Isaiah's writing. We find of dubious merit the suggestion that verse 5 is a comment on the unfaithfulness of the Jews as the children of God who have been cut off from Jerusalem.[45]

Isaiah uses the title "house" (fourteen times) more than "temple," as does Ezekiel (fifty-five times),[46] which may reflect the exilic experience where the people did not have a temple and worship was held in houses.[47] Further support for this idea is demonstrated by the references to houses in the Deuteronomistic material of Jeremiah.[48] We note that references to "house" as temple in Ezekiel are all in material (chs. 8–12, 40–48) that is regarded by Zimmerli and Biggs as very late.[49] The specific phrase in verse 7, "house of prayer," is exclusive to these verses and will be discussed later.

The literary structure of the passage presents God in a particular way: for example, my Sabbaths (56:4), my holy mountain (56:7; 57:13; 65:11, 25; 66:20), my house of prayer (56:7, 7), my altar (56:7), the place of my feet (60:13), my covenant (56:4,

---

[44] Orlinsky, "Nationalism-Universalism and Internationalism in Ancient Israel," believes it is "a deliberate play on *karuth*," "one whose member (or testicles) is cut off." In Isaiah 56:5 "an everlasting name which will never be cut off (lit.)," 222.

[45] J.D.W. Watts, *Isaiah 34–66,* 248.

[46] Isaiah uses "house" in 2:2, 3; 6:4; 37:1, 14; 38:20, 22; 56:5, 7; 60:7; 64:11; 66:1, 20 and "temple" in 6:1; 13:22; 44:28; 66:6. Biggs, "The Role of the Temple in the Book of Ezekiel," (unpublished Article presented to the Adelaide Theological Circle). Ezekiel uses "house" for Temple in forty-nine places and "house of Yahweh" six times.

[47] J. D. Newsome, *By the Waters of Babylon,* 81, 96.

[48] All references to the "house" as Temple (13x) and as "house of the Lord" (31x) are in the prose sermons of Jeremiah.

[49] Biggs, "The Role of *nasi . . .,*" 16. Zimmerli, *Ezekiel 1,* 73, 253.

6). In each case it serves to deepen the association of YHWH with the Temple, holy mountain, and his offer of relationship through his covenant.

יד, usually meaning "hand," is translated in its technical sense as monument or memorial by most authors in this instance.[50] A person's name is usually continued through their progeny, but the promise to the eunuch proclaims that his name will be perpetuated within the Temple and will never be blotted out. This promise is exceptional in light of the laws concerning those who are blemished. Someone who has been rejected and denied any access to the Temple is now acceptable and honored by God.[51] A parallel example of a person's name perpetuated through a monument is in 2 Samuel 18:18 where Absalom set up a monument because he had no son to keep his name in remembrance. The difference in Isaiah 56:5 is that God gives the promise of a monument. Therefore, it will have the divine authority to ensure its occurrence. Unlike Absalom, the eunuch has not set it up for himself.

The phrase יד ושם (a monument and a name) is unique in the Hebrew Scriptures.[52] Progeny and the ability to continue one's family line are of crucial importance in Hebrew culture.[53] To

---

[50] F. Brown, S. R. Driver and C. A. Briggs, *The New Brown-Driver-Briggs*, 390.4, Scullion, "Studies in Isaiah cc. 56–66," 106, Sekine, *Die Tritojesajanische Sammlung (Jes 56–66)*, 35, Pauritsch, *Die Neue Gemeinde*, 36, Whybray, *Isaiah 40–66*, 198. G. Robinson, "The Meaning of יד in Isaiah 56:5," suggests the phrase can be translated as "a possession and a share" and "name" refers to Genesis 12:2, Deuteronomy 25:6 (et al), while "hand" refers to Genesis 25:14; 43:34; Exodus 10:25, 282–84. If this connection is valid it would identify the eunuchs with the promise made to Abraham and further emphasize the everlasting nature of their inclusion with the people of God.

[51] Orlinsky, "Nationalism-Universalism and Internationalism in Ancient Israel," says the purpose of Isaiah 56:4-5 is to legalize the castrated Gentiles for sacred work in the Temple, 220.

[52] Robinson, "The Meaning of יד in Isaiah 56:5," 282–84.

[53] The promise to Abraham in Genesis 12:1-3 becomes a major part of the story which demonstrates how the action and promises of God can be fulfilled despite seemingly impossible odds, i.e., Sarah's age. Abraham's offspring become the nation of Israel.

suggest in that cultural context that God's monument to them will be better than one's own sons and daughters is unprecedented. God offers a hope that transcends all human activity, further verified by the promise in verse 5b (I will give them an everlasting name which shall not be cut off)[54] that, with the inclusion of the phrase in verse 5a makes the verse quite explicit. The Isaiah Targum not only retains the phrase "better than sons and daughters" but makes the message quite explicit with its interpretation: "I will give them in my sanctuary and within the land of my shekinah's house a place and a name. . . ."[55]

To summarize, there is a special offer to each group (eunuchs v. 4, foreigners v. 6a) that picks up their own particular concern and addresses it. Eunuchs will have an everlasting name, despite their physical inability to have progeny, and foreigners can minister to God, despite the laws that exclude them. Only if verses 3-5 are considered in isolation could we agree that the eunuchs are solely concerned with their lack of posterity.[56] However, in the context of verses 1-8 the eunuchs are not only promised posterity but also membership within the assembly (v. 7).

We note the three consequences for the foreigners who have joined themselves to the Lord. The literary structure of verses 6-7 compared with verses 4-5 has both similarities and differences.[57]

---

[54] Sekine, *Die Tritojesajanische Sammlung (Jes 56–66)*, argues for a chiastic structure of the plural (them) in verses 4 and 7 to the singular in verse 3, thereby supporting the argument for a deliberate structuring of verses 3-7, 40. He is not convinced by Volz that verse 5b ought to be in the singular, "to him" as depicted in the Masoretic Text.

[55] B. D. Chilton, *The Isaiah Targum*, 109.

[56] Whybray, *Isaiah 40–66*, considers the eunuchs are not converts with a desire to be admitted to the religious assembly, but are solely concerned with their lack of posterity, 198. Orlinsky, "Nationalism-Universalism and Internationalism in Ancient Israel," takes the opposite position, 220. He believes the eunuchs who have returned to Jerusalem from Babylon are seeking entry into temple service.

[57] Sekine, *Die Tritojesajanische Sammlung (Jes 56–66)*, compares verse 6aα with verse 3aα—singular to plural; verse 6bα is almost identical with verse 2bα; verse 6bβ is identical with verses 4b, 35.

Each group is addressed with conditions (eunuchs v. 4, foreigners v. 6a) and benefits (eunuchs v. 5, everyone v. 7). The difference appears in verse 6b that states that "everyone" who keeps the three requirements will receive the benefits in verse 7. This makes it important to read verses 1-8 as a whole or we miss the theological significance.

According to Whybray, when the phrase "who join themselves to the Lord" is applied to the foreigners, it must automatically include circumcision, even when circumcision is not mentioned explicitly in any of the conditions.[58] This argument from silence is based on a number of texts (Gen 17:9-14; Exod 12:44, 48; Lev 12:3; Ezek 44:7-9), and therefore Whybray assumes that the foreigners are circumcised. By not including this condition, the writer of Isaiah 56:1-8 faces increased difficulties in getting his message accepted when circumcision is an explicit requirement in Ezekiel. Not only is Trito-Isaiah promoting acceptance of foreigners within the worshiping community, but he fails to require circumcision as a condition.

Do the texts which talk of circumcision of the heart (Lev 26:41; Deut 10:16, 30:6; Jer 4:4, 6:10, 9:24) change the demand for the physical circumcision and become a means of avoiding the Law?[59] If we accept this suggestion, physical circumcision is not a necessary requirement for the foreigner and eunuch. In joining themselves to the Lord and keeping the laws, the circumcision of the heart is part of the foreigner's and eunuch's faith response. This argument, like Whybray's, is an argument from silence, and we do not know whether either of these cases was part of the author's thinking. But, we note how Ezekiel 44:7, 9 denies admittance to foreigners uncircumcised in heart and flesh. For Ezekiel, to be circumcised in the heart implies obedience to the Law. However, because uncircumcised foreigners were excluded from worship and therefore unable to hear the edicts of the Law, they will continue to be uncircumcised in heart.

[58] Whybray, *Isaiah 40–66*, 198.

[59] Sehmsdorf's, "Studien zur Redaktionsgeschicte von Jesaja 56–66," argument is based on the statement, "that it is no accident the above change is present in DT-DTR and Chr material," 546.

The foreigners who have joined the Lord are able to function in ways that previously had been the privilege of the Israelites alone (v. 6b): to minister, to love the name of the Lord, and to be his servants. לשרתו (to minister to him) is found frequently in Ezekiel and Chronicles but is absent from Deutero-Isaiah. BDB shows that the functions of this verb (שרת, minister) mainly involve service in the Temple and worship life. Numbers 18:1ff. has been suggested as a direct connection to 56:1-8 in which similar forms of service are performed by the Levites (v. 2, may minister to you, vv. 3-4, 6, will attend to the service of the tent while Aaron's house will attend to the priestly duties, v. 7). This connection is used to support a Levitical authorship for Isaiah 56:1-8.[60] On return from exile the Levitical priests are asserting their rights to be associated with the temple service.[61] The opposition to foreigners and eunuchs in Ezekiel and Nehemiah prohibits us from accepting Levitical or priestly authorship. Instead, we argue for a deliberate use of these terms in connection with the foreigners, thereby confronting the orthodox position of the day. The writer was aware that he was challenging the legal giants, Ezekiel and Nehemiah, when he used these functional terms in Isaiah 56:6a.

Other references using the term "to minister to him" (לשרתו) are always in the context of high positions in government. This serves to reinforce our suggestion that the clause is "an oxymoron," because it is the converse of the menial and slave-like service spoken of elsewhere for foreigners (Isaiah 60–62). Consequently, the message proclaimed in v. 6ab allows foreigners to serve the Lord in the Temple and as equals to the Israelites.

Despite the lack of comment by scholars, we propose that the employment of שרת (to serve) has significant theological

[60] Orlinsky, "Nationalism-Universalism and Internationalism in Ancient Israel," 222. Because of the connections to Numbers 18:1ff., the emphasis on Sabbath observance and the legalization of castrated Jews for sacred work in the Temple, Isaiah presents the interest of the priestly group in power in post-exilic times. Orlinsky denies the inclusive nature of Isaiah 56:1-8 and presents statements, but not the argument for his position, 221.

[61] Ibid., Orlinsky admits there are problems with his thesis. He is not sure when the Levitical priests became a separate identity or the role they played in post-exilic times, 222.

importance in view of the express command in Ezekiel against the admission of foreigners to the Temple (44:7, 9).[62] Evidently foreigners had been allowed previously to serve in the Temple (Ezek 44:8), but now Ezekiel declares that no foreigner shall be admitted.

In the Ezekiel writings only Levites (44:1) and Zadokites (44:15-31) are able to minister, whereas the foreigner is expressly named as the one to minister in Isaiah 56:1-8. The knowledge that Ezekiel is reacting against a practice that has occurred already in the worship life of Israel (Ezek 44:8) indicates an acceptance by some people of this custom. It further supports our thesis that Ezekiel and Nehemiah are reacting to this practice with their strong exclusive statements. In response Trito-Isaiah writes a polemic on behalf of those who are threatened with expulsion.

"His servants" in Isaiah 65–66 are those people who are faithful to the Lord, whereas in 56:6 the servants are the foreigners who have become followers of YHWH. Are these two groups of people the ones who will constitute the community of YHWH? In the Hebrew Scriptures, prior to Isaiah 56:6, only the Israelites (Lev 25:55, "For it is to Me the Israelites are servants") and Nebuchadnezzar (Jer 25:9, 27:6, 43:10) had been designated God's servants. The designation of "servants" given to the foreigners appears to be part of the deliberate structuring of Isaiah 56–66 where "servants" becomes an overarching theme.

The author continues to employ concepts that in past writings referred only to the Israelite people. The functions remarked on above, "to minister to him," "to love the name of the Lord," and "to be his servants," are a deliberate construction by the writer. He is announcing a changed understanding of community.

The proclamation changes at this point with an expansion in the passage to include everyone who "keeps the Sabbath, and

---

[62] Zimmerli, *Ezekiel 2*, believes that the attitude to foreigners in 56:3-8 contradicts that expressed in Ezekiel 44 and we note that it is the only place in Ezekiel that uses the root נכר. We see from reading Ezekiel 44 the concern of the prophet to purify what he sees as an abomination to the Lord, i.e., the foreigners' service in the Temple, 453.

does not profane it, and holds fast my covenant." Two specific groups of people are spoken of in verses 3-6a, but in 6b-8 the message is expanded to include all people who keep the Sabbath and hold fast to God's covenant. The strong emphasis on obedience here recalls similar emphases by the Deuteronomic writers who call for obedience to the Mosaic Law. In this passage the first requirement is to keep the Sabbath and then hold fast to the covenant; this order corresponds to other exilic texts which put the Sabbath as primary.

Verse 6 has an arresting list of verbs: "join," "minister," "love," "be," "keep," "profane," "holds fast." All are pro-active with "profane" alone carrying a negative sense. All are activities which people, both foreigners and "everyone," are exhorted to do. The consequences of these actions are proclaimed in verse 7. God himself states these consequences which follow the same pattern as in verse 4, the exhortation, and verse 5, the personal response of God.

"Them" (v. 7) refers back to "everyone" in verse 6b and therefore all the people mentioned in the previous verses. The hiphil of בוא (to come, hiphil = to bring) suggests they are not yet in Jerusalem; "to bring" usually has the connotation that someone has to be moved physically from one space to another.[63] The difficulty arises when verse 3 sounds as though the foreigners are already in Jerusalem and verse 7 suggests they are still to come. There is no easy answer to this problem. Other references in the Hebrew Scriptures (for example, Jer 3:14; Neh 1:9; Ps 78:54; Exod 15:17) use the root בוא (to bring) exclusively of the Israelite people who will be brought back to the mountain by YHWH. In addition, YHWH brings the Israelites out of Egypt (Ezek 20:35, 42; 34:13). This statement which declares

---

[63] Pauritsch, *Die Neue Gemeinde,* notes that the importance is certainly in the hiphil, "I will bring"; the subject will bring a person or thing from one situation to another (Gen 43:17; Hag 1:6) 36. Sekine, *Die Tritojesajanische Sammlung (Jes 56–66),* believes that verse 3 implies that the foreigners are already part of the YHWH congregation, but in verse 7 they are standing outside and only in the future will be brought to the Holy mountain, 36. This argument is not conclusive when quotes are being used in verse 3 to make the point.

that God brings the foreigners to Jerusalem as he once brought the Israelites out of Egypt demonstrates God's freedom to act in new and controversial ways.

Verse 7 is the one place in the Hebrew Scriptures where the Temple is referred to as בבית תפלתי (my house of prayer, v. 7a, b). Such a title may reflect the people's stay in Babylon where an emphasis on prayer replaced the emphasis on the Temple and sacrificial worship. The prayer of Solomon from the Deuteronomic historian in 1 Kings 8:27-53 gives support to this suggestion because most commentators place these verses in exile.[64] In 1 Kings 8:41-43 YHWH is petitioned to answer the foreigner (נכר) who has come to the Temple (house) to pray. YHWH is expected to answer the foreigner's prayer in order that all the peoples of the earth will know of YHWH and the Temple of God (v. 43). It must be a significant relationship for the foreigner to command such power with YHWH.

We note one significant similarity between Isaiah 56:7 and the texts which speak about nations coming to Jerusalem (1 Kgs 8:41-43; Isa 2:1-4; Mic 4:1-5; Zech 8:20-23). Each passage speaks of people or nations coming to Jerusalem to learn of God's way or to seek his favor. However, only Isaiah 56:1-8 states explicitly the status of the foreigner within the worshipping community of Israel. The conditions for acceptance into the community are the same as for the Israelites (Isa 56:4b, 6b) and the foreigners have an equal status within the worshipping community (Isa 56:5, 6a, 7).

None of the texts refers to a "house of prayer" although the context of 1 Kings 8:41-43—they pray towards "this house"—suggests that this passage has a much closer connection with

---

[64] F. M. Cross, Jr. "The Themes of the Book of Kings and the Structure of the Deuteronomistic History," in whose analysis verses 41-43 are included in the pre-exilic material which makes the attitude to foreigners very liberal for pre-exilic material, 287. S. J. DeVries *1 Kings,* believes that this is the most universalistic passage in the Hebrew Scriptures, 126. B. O. Long, *1 Kings with an Introduction to Historical Literature,* 94. M. Noth, *Deuteronomistic History,* 91ff. N. H. Snaith, "The First and Second Books of Kings," believes the exilic editor made considerable interpolations into the prayer in 1 Kings 8, but does not designate particular verses, 11.

Isaiah 56:7 than the others. A further similarity between Isaiah 56:7 and 1 Kings 8:41-43 is the use of נכר (foreigner) as opposed to the normal word גוי (nation) used in the other texts. In 1 Kings 8:41-43 the foreigner's prayer will be heard by YHWH. Nevertheless, there are distinct differences which create a new message in Isaiah 56:1-8.

One passage in Kings, three in the book of Isaiah, and a possible parallel in Micah are insufficient evidence to establish with accuracy the extent to which the nations ever participated as equals in the life of the Israelite people. However, the condemnatory statement in Ezekiel 44:7 suggests that for a period of time some foreigners were equal participants in the worship life of Israel. So this text, together with those mentioned above, supports the view that at some stage in the life of Israel foreigners were able to play an active role within the worship life of the community.

This particular designation of the Temple as a "house of prayer" acts as an *inclusio* around the statement that their burnt offerings and sacrifices will be acceptable (7ab). The Temple is a place both of prayer and of sacrificial worship (v. 7). All people will be able to bring "their burnt offerings" to the altar, and the Temple will be a "house of prayer" for all peoples. Ezekiel 44:7, 9 speaks strongly against the admittance of foreigners to the sanctuary, illustrating the radical nature of the proclamation in Isaiah 56:6-7.[65]

Not only are the sacrifices of foreigners acceptable and therefore blessed, but the house of prayer is for all peoples. Westermann goes as far as to suggest that since their sacrifice is acceptable they cease to be foreigners.[66] Even the Targum that is predisposed to theological conservatism retains the translation "for all the peoples."[67]

In summary, the exhortation to the foreigners includes a relationship with God (v. 6b) that is both unexpected and exceptional in light of previous restrictions imposed on foreigners

---

[65] עלה (burnt offering) is found frequently in the law codes and post-exilic writings, which further supports a post-exilic dating for Isaiah 56:1-8.

[66] Westermann, *Isaiah 40–66*, 315.

[67] Chilton, *The Isaiah Targum*, 109.

(Ezekiel 44). They have the same rights and privileges as the Israelites and the exhortation of verse 6a, b is extended to everyone, with the primary stipulation to keep Sabbath holiness followed by the demands of "my covenant" (v. 6b).

Verses 6-7 repeat the same pattern as 4-5 where 5 and 7 proclaim God's actions in response to the exhortations in 4 and 6. God will bring the foreigners, the eunuchs, and the Israelites to Jerusalem and into the Temple, named here as "my house of prayer," in which everyone will participate fully in the sacrificial life of the community. Isaiah 56:7 appears to be the only place in the Hebrew Scriptures in which we find such a clear and overt message about the inclusion of non-Israelites in the Israelite community.

The opening phrase of verse 8 is usually the closing formula of an inspired speech. It gives authority to the preceding words (vv. 1-7), intending them to be understood as divine revelation. Indeed, the controversial message discussed above requires the authority of God for its release from past prohibitions that were sacred to Israel. The conflict between people is apparent. One group calls on sacred Scripture to support their position, and another group believes God's revelation breaks people free from earlier laws that now bind the community.

God gathers the outcasts of Israel, without any explicit conditions attached. קבץ (to gather together), when it is linked with the "scattered ones," has become an exclusive word of salvation.[68] This interpretation is supported in BDB when the piel form of קבץ is translated "to gather in" the dispersed peoples who can be both Israelites and foreigners.[69] The concept of "gathering" is an activity which is assigned to God in other places without this specific verb employed; for example, a shepherd who is symbolic of "God gathering in" is mentioned

---

[68] Pauritsch, *Die Neue Gemeinde,* 38, Sekine, *Die Tritojesajanische Sammlung (Jes 56–66),* 36. A study of other places in the Hebrew Scriptures which speak of the outcasts returning home has Zion as the goal either directly or indirectly, thus reinforcing the destination in verse 7. Isaiah 11:12 gathers the outcasts from Judah and Israel.

[69] F. Brown, S. R. Driver and C. A. Briggs, *The New Brown-Driver-Briggs,* 868.

explicitly in Jeremiah 23, Ezekiel 34, and Isaiah 40:11. Here is a God who acts solely out of his own compassion without conditions attached.

In verse 8a the promise is to the "outcasts of Israel" (usual English translation of the "scattered ones"), which could mean the exiles of both the Northern and Southern Kingdoms (Isa 11:12).

An examination of Psalm 147:2 finds the same phrase (outcasts of Israel) is used in parallel with "the Lord builds up Jerusalem." Further reading of the passage speaks of God binding up the brokenhearted and healing the wounded. There seems no reason to read Psalm 147:2 as referring to the true descendants of the old northern Israel, pre 721 B.C.E. It reads equally well in reference to the people who have returned from the Babylonian exile. In Isaiah 11:12 the phrase (outcasts of Israel) is part of a context in which YHWH is recovering the remnant from across a number of countries (v. 11), including the dispersed of Judah. In this context the writer is referring to the exiles of the Assyrian defeat in 721 B.C.E. Later in Hebrew Scriptures the term "Israel" became a theological term, meaning all the people who were regarded as the people of God.[70] Kaiser says while verse 10 refers to the nations coming to seek the root of Jesse, the context of Isaiah 11:12 suggests the ensign raised in the nations will be a sign for the dispersed of Judah to gather,[71] or the outcasts in Isaiah 56:8a that include eunuchs and foreigners.[72]

---

[70] Zimmerli, *Ezekiel 2*, (Appendix 2), argues that Israel refers to the whole people of God whether they are in Babylon or Jerusalem/Judah, 563–65.

[71] O. Kaiser, *Isaiah 1–12*, 264–68. Clements, *Isaiah 1–39*, 125. R.B.Y. Scott, "The Book of Isaiah," 152. Scullion, "Studies in Isaiah cc. 56–66," 159. Both Scott and Clements maintain this is a post-exilic prophecy, fourth century, referring to the Diaspora.

[72] Pauritsch, *Die Neue Gemeinde*, 38. Pauritsch names the following texts to support his view that YHWH is gathering all people including eunuchs and foreigners, Isaiah 11:12; Jeremiah 29:14; 32:37; Ezekiel 34:13; Micah 4:6; Zephaniah 3:19; Deuteronomy 30:4; Nehemiah 1:9. Except for Micah 4:6, the remaining texts speak of either Israel or Judah as the ones who will be gathered back and do not refer to people of other nations. If Micah 4:6 was taken in isolation, one would suggest it refers only to those who have

Verse 8b is the subject of disagreement among scholars. Is God intending to gather other exiles to join those who are already gathered in Jerusalem or is God intending to gather "others" who are not of Israelite descent? The answer to the question is based on the interpretation of the verb קבץ (to gather), which for some scholars means an exclusive gathering of Israelites, particularly the Babylonian exiles.[73] Kessler narrows the interpretation of the "scattered" to mean the dispersed people of the Northern Kingdom.[74] His argument for this proposal is based on Isaiah 2:2, which he believes is a direct parallel to Isaiah 56:8.

We accept the words as they stand in verse 8b that God intends to gather the foreigners and eunuchs mentioned in verses 3-7.[75] God will continue his purposes by reaching out to non-Israelites. This inclusive interpretation is congruent with the theology presented in verses 1-7.

Pauritsch, Scullion, and Whybray agree that verse 8 was a separate oracle that has been put here deliberately, to conclude the word of God begun in verse 1.[76] The context in which the verse now stands and the radical message in verses 1-7 clearly

---

been taken into exile, but in the context of the whole chapter it is possible to see this as part of a continuing message to the nations. Because Micah 4:6 appears ambiguous, scholars have a divided opinion on the status of the foreigners who come up to Zion. Consequently, on reading the references one cannot support Pauritsch, for the "nations" are the places from which the Israelites will return.

[73] Smart, *History and Theology in Second Isaiah*, 237.

[74] Scullion, "Studies in Isaiah cc. 56–66," refers to Kessler, 159. This particular article by Kessler was not available to me.

[75] Scullion, "Studies in Isaiah cc. 56–66," says that "to these his own who have now at last been gathered together, YHWH will add still more foreigners, eunuchs, those who seem to be beyond the pale of the assembly," 160. Pauritsch, *Die Neue Gemeinde*, agrees with Scullion, "the author has obviously the eunuchs and outsiders in view," 38. Blenkinsopp "Second Isaiah—Prophet of Universalism," says it is "a comment on Isaiah 11:12 which is updated to include Gentiles," 95. Muilenburg, "Isaiah Chapters 40–66," 659, Westermann, *Isaiah 40–66*, 315.

[76] Pauritsch, *Die Neue Gemeinde*, 31. Whybray, *Isaiah 40–66*, 199. Scullion "Studies in Isaiah cc. 56–66," 158–59.

dictates that God is gathering not only the Israelites (v. 8a) but also the foreigners (v. 8b). The verse (56:8) becomes a summary of God's comprehensive purpose which is to gather all those who accept the Law and covenant—exiles and foreigners. However, our position is that verse 8 is part of this passage (vv. 1-8) although it may have a history of use in other contexts.

We argued earlier in the chapter that the phrase "thus says the Lord" gives authority to the statements which follow in 56:1a, 4a, 8a. This is of particular importance in view of the radical suggestions contained in verses 1-8: that is, YHWH accepts foreigners, eunuchs, and others into the community who will keep the requirements in verses 4b and 6b. Although verse 8b may have referred to the Israelites in past contexts in the Hebrew Scriptures, the present position of the verse requires that it is interpreted within the framework and content of verses 1-7.

In the exegesis above we have made some tentative connections to material that is usually regarded as late post-exilic. If Trito-Isaiah is writing an apologetic polemic against Ezra/ Nehemiah and Ezekiel, we need to say something of the historical context into which this proclamation is addressed. What happened to cause such radical changes in thinking and be in opposition to the orthodox views on inclusion? Change sometimes occurs in people's thinking when they reflect on their experience in life. In this case it may be reflection by a group of people who have accepted foreigners. They want to include them as equals in their community, despite opposition by those who seek only to have a community of "bloodline" Israelites.[77]

Contemporary scholarship has failed to achieve any consensus on the date of Isaiah 56:1-8, either when it was written or when it became part of Isaiah 1–66. The first suggested period for their composition is immediately after the return of the exiles to Jerusalem, around 530–520 B.C.E.[78] Those people who

---

[77] "Community" in this context is the Israelite people who have accepted YHWH as their God and membership of this community is basically by biological descent. A few slaves may have been accepted as part of families, but they would not have received the same privileges as the Israelites.

[78] O. Eissfeldt, *The Old Testament,* trans. P. R. Ackroyd, 344. N. H. Snaith, "Isaiah 40–66," 967. W. S. McCullough, "A Re-examination of Isaiah 56–66,"

remained in Jerusalem during the exilic period had a quite different experience from those who went into exile in Babylon.[79] In 598, 587, and 582 B.C.E. (Jer 52:28-30), the Babylonians deported significant numbers of Israelites to Babylon, especially the leaders and highly educated people, which meant that those left behind were bereft of leadership (Lamentations 2, 4, 5). Cultic activity continued at many centers, including the destroyed Temple (2 Kgs 25:9-15), presided over by lower orders of priests (2 Kgs 25:18-21; Jer 41:5).[80] We infer from these writings that the religious practices became lax at this time owing to the depletion of priestly and prophetic leadership. Ahlström and Gottwald believe that many neighboring people were allowed to encroach on the territory of Judah.[81] As a result, the community included people of different nationalities. This community may have allowed mixed marriages and the inclusion of eunuchs, with consequent laxity in the observation of the Mosaic Law. Only tentative conclusions can be drawn about the situation in Jerusalem because of a lack of historical knowledge about the conditions in Judah from the 582 B.C.E. deportation, following the assassination of Gedeliah, until the return of the Babylonian exiles, circa 538 B.C.E.

It is easier to obtain information about the exiles in Babylon than about the conditions for those who remained in the land (Judah). We have both biblical sources and inscriptions found in Mesopotamia on which to draw. It appears that the Babylonians allowed the exiles to own land (Jer 29:5) and gave them much freedom. They could continue to worship (Ezek 8:1; 14:1, 3; 20:1, 29; Jer 29:1), to participate in trade (Marashu business texts), to remain in tribal groups with their leaders (Jer 29:5-7), and to serve on royal projects and in the military forces. The

---

27–36. McCullough is the exception to the date suggested above. He maintains that Isaiah 56–66 came from a Palestinian school of Isaianic prophets dated 587–562 B.C.E., 27. Isaiah 40–55 comes after 56–66, 36.

[79] J. H. Hayes and J. M. Miller, *Israelite and Judaean History,* 476–80. J. M. Miller and J. H. Hayes, *A History of Ancient Israel and Judah,* 426. Ackroyd, *Exile and Restoration,* 21–31.

[80] N. K. Gottwald, *The Hebrew Bible: A Socio-Literary Introduction,* 425.

[81] G. W. Ahlström, *The History of Ancient Palestine from the Palaeolithic Period to Alexander's Conquest,* 822–47.

evidence of the Jeremiah, Deutero-Isaiah, Ezekiel, and Priestly material showed that writing and reworking of the traditions to speak to a new situation continued in the exile. An awareness of both the written and oral traditions of the past is seen in these books. While some writings (Deutero-Isaiah, Jeremiah, Deuteronomic History) probably received their final form in exile, other writings (Priestly, Psalms, Ezekiel) did not achieve their final form until much later. The people were aware of the Torah requirements (see Lev 26:14-45, an exilic sermon), and Ezekiel drew upon the laws in the Holiness Code in Leviticus 17–25.[82] The later writings confirmed that the people in Babylon knew the requirements of the Law (Ezra 7:11-20: Ezra the priest, the scribe of the Law, the one sent by the God of heaven to Jerusalem with treasures for the Temple and a commission to undertake teaching of the Law and moral reform). We assume that if Ezra was going to Jerusalem as a teacher of the Law, he would also have been teaching the Law to those in Babylon. In summary, the exilic community appears to have been well organized, able to enjoy the benefits of Babylonian life, and free to maintain its own religious life and worship. Although the people were not able to worship at the Temple and offer sacrifices, they learned about their past traditions (Isaiah 40–55) and the requirements of the Law (Deuteronomic History, Ezekiel, Leviticus).

Though no direct evidence of the conditions and events following the return of the exiles is available, tentative comments can be made about their political, religious, and social life. Disagreement between the returned exiles who were keen to uphold the strict Torah requirements and those who remained in the land (Judah) would have occurred if the exiles found that strangers and eunuchs were accepted into the worshipping community.[83]

---

[82] C. R. Biggs in his thesis believes that the basic form of H was thus achieved in the exilic period, that is, its laws were intended for the exilic community, and were the subject of preaching in that period, "Exegesis in the book of Ezekiel: A Study of the Development of earlier Biblical material in the sermonic passages in the book," 356–57.

[83] D. Smith, *The Religion of the Landless: The Social Context of the Babylonian Exile*, 35–37.

The infiltration of other peoples may have caused those remaining in Jerusalem to be more receptive of strangers within their community. Because of this experience, Isaiah 56:1-8 may come from the period directly after the return from exile. On the other hand, eunuchs who served at the court in Babylon may have converted to the faith of the exiles and after returning with the exilic groups found themselves excluded from worship. There is no evidence that foreigners and eunuchs were part of the worshiping community in exile. The stress on the Holiness Code makes it difficult to imagine that eunuchs were admitted into the Israelite community when the Law explicitly condemned them (Lev 22:10-16). The importance of the Law and its strict requirements about eunuchs suggest that the inclusive proclamation came from the group of people who had been left in the land.

However, while Isaiah 56:1-8 may reflect the experience of a community around 500 B.C.E. we are suggesting the possibility that Trito-Isaiah was writing much closer to 400 B.C.E., if not later, and using earlier traditions which were adapted to speak to a crisis situation brought on by the proclamations of Ezra/Nehemiah and Ezekiel.

Summary of 56:1-8

Our examination of Isaiah 56:1-8 leads us to assert that it was intentionally compiled by Trito-Isaiah to proclaim God's word in a crisis situation. He realized the need for a new and radical message. The structure itself was a means of emphasizing specific theological pronouncements. For example, verses 1-2 are written intentionally to introduce the issue of justice and righteousness. This issue becomes specific to two groups of people in verses 3-7 and inclusive of all people in verses 6b-8. Righteousness and justice are the theological base for Trito-Isaiah's assertion that foreigners and eunuchs could be members with "full voting rights" within the Israelite community.

Verse 2 is the hinge verse between the exhortation and promise of verse 1 and further detailed exhortation and promises that are addressed to the specific groups of foreigners and eunuchs in verses 3-8. The placement of the phrase, "Thus says the Lord," in verses 1a, 4a, and 8a serves to give authority to the exceptional message which follows. The earlier parallel pattern of verses 4-5 and 6-7 has been noted. Verses 4 and 6 entreat the eunuchs (v. 4) "to keep my Sabbaths, choose things that please me, hold fast my covenant" and foreigners (v. 6) "to join themselves to the Lord, to minister to him, to love him and to be his servants," followed in each case by specific promises of God to the eunuchs in verse 5 and the foreigners in verse 7. We have the unconditional promises of God and in response the obligations of those people—Israelites, foreigners, eunuchs —who will do what is required in verses 4 and 6.

Verse 8 not only gathers up the message of the previous verses, but also points us forward to Isaiah 66:18-24. It is our argument that verses 1-8 are structured intentionally, both as the opening prologue and as an integral part of chapters 56–66.

We named another literary method employed by Trito-Isaiah as "an oxymoron." This happens when the writer takes a particular theological understanding, turns it around, and uses it against the current thinking of the day. We found this phenomenon several times in Isaiah 56:1-8 in which familiar understandings have been taken and turned against the orthodox position prevalent at the time. It occurs in verses 3, 4, 5, 6, and 8. In verse 3 statements by the eunuch (v. 3c) and by the foreigner (v. 3b) are contrary to the Mosaic Law and to the Holiness code. We are challenged especially to realize the significance of the statement by the foreigner who is not allowed to say he is separate from God's people.

In many of the examples mentioned above we have noted how the message was the converse of that in Ezekiel and Nehemiah. This difference in theological position will be examined in more detail in chapter 5.

We suggest a date around 400 B.C.E. for the composition of these verses. This is in agreement with those scholars who see the writing in response to the edicts of Ezra/Nehemiah. We include also the writing of Ezekiel as instrumental in provoking the rebuttal we see in Isaiah 56:1-8.[84] The conflicting views on

---

[84] Snaith, "Isaiah 40–66," disagrees with the date (420–400 B.C.E.) which we have set for both the Ezekiel material and Isaiah 56–66. He believes

who is included in the worshiping community and who is excluded is strongly pronounced in all these books. We have noted how particular theological concepts used exclusively of the relationship of YHWH to Israel in the writings of Ezekiel ("to profane," "to minister, to love, to serve"), Ezra/Nehemiah (to separate) apply now to the foreigners in Isaiah 56:1-8.

Our tentative suggestions about the author, Trito-Isaiah, see him writing a possible polemic in response to the reforms of Ezekiel, Ezra/Nehemiah in post-exilic Judah. We spoke earlier in this chapter about a group who might be in danger of exclusion from the community. This group could be the ones left in Judah, which gradually included foreigners who moved into the territories to fill the vacuum left by the deportation of the exiles. Trito-Isaiah is breaking new ground in his call to include foreigners and eunuchs who are normally excluded. Like the prophetic voices of the past he confronts the authorities of his day. Whereas the prophets were speaking only to and for the Israelite people, Trito-Isaiah speaks on behalf of Israelites and foreigners, which broadens the boundaries of who can and who cannot belong in the worshiping community. Later we shall see how the criteria for belonging to YHWH narrows to exclude those Israelites who are unfaithful and commit apostasy. There was always the sense with previous prophetic utterances that, despite Israel's disobedience, YHWH still called them his people. Isaiah 65 and 66 confront this assumption.

We are able to conclude that Isaiah 56:1-8 presents a message which many would have found heretical and blasphemous in their interpretation of the Law. Particularly, we discussed the new form of exhortation and promise: the justice and righteousness of God as extended to all people who keep the Sabbath and the covenant; eunuchs are given a special hope quite contradictory to the Abrahamic promise; everyone who is faithful is able to serve within the worshiping community; God will continue to seek and gather in others. This is a message which is unique not only in the book of Isaiah but also in the Hebrew Scriptures. In raising the significance of this passage

---

both were written in the same period (510–500 B.C.E.) after the return from Babylon and as part of a struggle for power, 227.

and suggesting it is part of a deliberate apologetic by the author we not only want people to see how important it is in the past but also its significance for us today.

2

•••••••••

Isaiah 56–66

We worked through the exegetical issues in some detail for Isaiah 56:1-8 in the last chapter. Our intention was to demonstrate the careful literary structure of the unit and the very clever use of oxymoron type features which confronted the people to hear this radical message. We believe that this argument for an inclusive community is carried through in the remainder of Isaiah 56–66 which culminates in the extraordinary inclusive message of Isaiah 66:18-24. These verses will also be examined in detail in order to make some observations about the inclusive nature of Isaiah 56–66.

We have not attempted to define possible earlier traditions and the *Sitz im Leben* of the traditions used in Isaiah 56–66. Many earlier scholars have given their time to this exercise and we give a summary of their positions in table I in the Appendix. We are interested in studying chapters 56–66 as a literary unit while recognizing that the creator of this material has appropriated earlier traditions.

What follows is a brief summary of the message in Isaiah 56:9–66:24 before we look at possible connections across the chapters.

After the inclusive message of Isaiah 56:1-8, an immediate impact is made by the stark pictures that describe the situation as perceived by the writer. Leaders have gone astray and hedonism is the way of life, according to the four verses which follow Isaiah 56:1-8. It is difficult to identify the shepherds who have "no understanding" (56:11), and we are unable to discern the particular situation in Israel to which this description refers. Furthermore, the metaphor of the dogs to describe those who should be watching is extremely derogatory.

Isaiah 57 spells out in detail the idolatrous behavior of the people: judgment will befall them and their adopted idols will not rescue them. Abruptly, verse 13b declares that those people who take shelter in God will receive the land. The ones who are humble and contrite will dwell in "the high and holy place" because God will cease to be angry. However, God excludes the wicked. Presumably the wicked are the Israelites who fail to keep in relationship with YHWH.

Isaiah 58 expounds the sins of the people even further. Moreover, the chapter combines two major areas of sinful behavior in the eyes of God: cultic impropriety and unethical behavior (vv. 1-7, 9b-10a, 13). If these behaviors are reversed, the people will be saved (vv. 8-9a, 10b-12, 14). As in Isaiah 56:1-8, a similar emphasis on the Sabbath occurs in this chapter. The separation from YHWH is blamed on the people's sinfulness which is described in graphic pictures in Isaiah 59:1-8 and reiterated by the people who acknowledge their sins in 59:9-15. In response the Lord will put on righteousness, with the result his enemies will suffer his anger and those who turn from their sins will be redeemed. The separation between the ungodly and the righteous, which is detailed in chapters 65–66, is pre-figured in both Isaiah 57 and 58. Included in the covenant which God will make with those who are faithful is the promise to the generations which follows: his spirit will remain with them evermore (Isa 59:21; cf. 66:22-23).

In Isaiah 60 the nations will come to Jerusalem because they see the light and the glory which God has bestowed on the city (60:3). Glory and light are used in parallel in 60:1 and 2, with the emphasis of God's glory constantly upon Zion. Further glory is achieved when the special timbers of Lebanon will be used to beautify the Temple (60:13). As chapter 60 begins with pronouncements about the manner of God's glory, so it finishes with further announcements that the city no longer needs natural light. Instead it is replaced by the light and glory of God. In Isaiah 62:2 even kings will see the glory of Zion, and this glory rests solely on Zion as the place where nations will see it and respond.

This response, as demonstrated in Isaiah 60:5, 6, 11, will bring the wealth of the nations for the use of Israel. Even their flocks will be acceptable on the altar of the Lord. The foreigners will acknowledge the descendants of Jerusalem and see them as blessed (61:9) and will never again have control of Israel's vineyards and food supplies (62:8). The role of the foreigners when they come to Jerusalem will be to build the walls. The kings also will serve Jerusalem (60:10). Aliens will become servants in the fields, do the ploughing, and tend the vineyards (61:5).

This brief overview of the role of the nations in Isaiah 60–62 demonstrates the subservience and inferior role that they will have within the Jerusalem community. They will be attracted by the glory surrounding Jerusalem which declares the power and majesty of YHWH. Both the glory which attracts them and their subsequent subordinate role are part of the hope that is offered to the exiles after their return from Babylon.

What perspective do these divergent pieces of literature represent for us? Isaiah 60–62 declares Zion as the place of peace, righteousness, wealth and prosperity, where God's glory is manifest. It is triumphant in its proclamation; there is an assurance of God's purposes coming to fruition; the Israelite people are favored and will reap all the benefits of God's actions. The nations' response acknowledges the power and glory of a God who does not bring them any benefits either materially or as participants within the worshiping community. In Isaiah 60–62 confidence and hope abound. As a vision of the future for the exiles it gives assurance, promise, and a picture of encouragement after their return. It was first written either just prior to their return from Babylon or soon after the arrival of the exiles in Jerusalem.[1] However, this picture never became a reality.

Isaiah 60–62 contains a strong emphasis on the role and place of Zion. The proclamation is unconditional and states how God will act towards Zion and his people. Images of light and glory rest on Zion which attract the foreigners. In response

---

[1] G. Emmerson, *Isaiah 56–66*, 59. J. Muilenburg, "Isaiah Chapters 40–66," 414. C. Westermann, *Isaiah 40–66*, 297. R. N. Whybray, *Isaiah 40–66*, 229.

the foreigners are wholly subordinate to Israel, a situation that gives honor to YHWH. God will make an everlasting covenant with the returned exiles and their descendants will be known among the nations (Isaiah 61). The people respond with their acknowledgment of what God will do, which includes the recognition of God's righteousness. The final verses of Isaiah 62 affirm the special relationship between YHWH, his people, and the city.

We move from God's promise of renewal and restoration in chapters 60–62 to the portrait of a God who is angry and vengeful in Isaiah 63:1-6. When God looks, there is no one to save. Here is one of many contradictions which the writer of Trito-Isaiah seems to have retained in Isaiah 56–66 (Isa 63:5, *I looked, but there was no one to uphold* versus a promise of renewal and restoration to the people, Isa 65:17). The sense of well-being and hope for the people of Israel is shattered when we read the opening verses of Isaiah 63:1-6.

The lament in Isaiah 63:7–64:11[2] has often been isolated by some from the rest of Isaiah 56–66 because of its form and its apparent exilic setting. References to the ruined state of Jerusalem and to the Temple are the primary reasons for this proposal (63:18, 64:10-11).[3] Because the intensity of the suffering is less than that described in Lamentations 2, a time later in exile rather than earlier is suggested for its origin.[4] We accept the

---

[2] The majority of commentators follow the Massoretic numbering of the verses in Isaiah 64 rather than that used in some English translations.

[3] Emmerson, *Isaiah 56–66*, 27. P. Hanson, *The Dawn of Apocalyptic*, 87. Muilenburg, "Isaiah Chapters 40–66," 729–30. K. Pauritsch, *Die Neue Gemeinde*, 169. Whybray, *Isaiah 40–66*, 256. H.G.M. Williamson, "Isa 63:7–64:11," 48–58.

[4] Hanson, *The Dawn of Apocalyptic*, believes the displaced Levitical priests are the complainants against the Zadokite party recently returned from exile in 520 B.C.E., 92. He is supported by E. Achtemeier, *The Community and Message of Isaiah 56–66*, 112. A. Aejmelaeus, "Der Prophet als Klageliedsänger Zur Funktion des Psalms Jes 63:7–64:11 in Tritojesaja," 31–50. J. Morgenstern sees this material as a response to the belief that the second Temple was destroyed in 485 B.C.E., "Isaiah 63:7-14," 185–203. Therefore, verses 7-14 were written around 460 B.C.E., 203. Muilenburg, "Isaiah Chapters 40–66," dates it 560–550 B.C.E., 730. J. J. Scullion, "Studies

strong possibility that this lament reflects an exilic setting, but like Williamson we believe it has been deliberately incorporated into Trito-Isaiah's composition at a much later date.

Because Isaiah 63:7–64:11 draws on the lament genre, the reader will be helped to touch into feelings of loss and grief, which reinforce the depth of feeling spoken of in the lament. Indeed, we note that there is lament (Isaiah 59) both prior to and following Isaiah 60–62. Do these laments somehow reflect disappointment because the ideal situation spoken of in 60–62 has never become a reality? We may be able to answer that question only in the literary sense noting how the creator of Isaiah 56–66 has chosen to place the two laments (Isaiah 59 and 63:7–64:11) either side of Isaiah 60–62. Furthermore, this is additional evidence that Isaiah 56–66 could be a literary unit, carefully structured to give a new and unique proclamation. Isaiah 63:7–64:11 also acts as a response to Isaiah 63:1-6 in which the vengeance of YHWH is announced in graphic terms.[5]

Isaiah 65:1-25 is perceived predominantly as a unified structure in its final form. How it came to be in its present form is still debatable. The possibility exists that we have a number of smaller units that were joined together, or alternatively there was a core (vv. 2-23) to which verses 1 and 24 were added later (v. 25 added at the same time as Isa 66:24).[6]

---

in Isaiah cc. 56–66," dates the lament between 538–515 B.C.E. when there has been time for the returnees to form a group but no ruler, no unified people and no temple to give cohesion, 181.

[5] E. W. Conrad, *Reading Isaiah*, 107. N. K. Gottwald, *The Hebrew Bible, A Socio-Literary Introduction*, suggests that Isaiah 56–66 had a deliberate literary structure in which Isaiah 60–62 were the central core around which material of similar kind was arranged in a deliberate literary formation, 508.

[6] E. C. Webster, "The Rhetoric of Isaiah 63–65," 96. Hanson, *The Dawn of Apocalyptic*, believes it is a "unit except for two minor additions," 135. Muilenburg, "Isaiah Chapters 40–66," 745. Pauritsch, *Die Neue Gemeinde*, 172. Pauritsch proposes that "vv. 2-23 are a teaching unity" with verse 1 and verse 24 as the future judgment brackets and verse 25 a later apocalyptic addition, 173, 177. Whybray, *Isaiah 40–66*, regards the chapter as composed from a number of smaller units, 267.

Chapter 65:1-25[7] is structured around the theme of YHWH saying, "I was available to my people, I was rejected and I shall create new heavens and a new earth for those who are faithful." God desired a relationship with his chosen people, Israel. But, when God said, "Here am I," the people continued to turn away and go after other gods. Indeed, the list of cultic sins of which they are accused leaves us in no doubt about the apostasy and faithlessness of YHWH's chosen. There is a sense of both sorrow and indignity that is expressed by the repeated "when I called, you did not answer" (65:1, 12), compared with the feeling of hope when God announces he will answer the faithful before they call (65:24). This group for whom God will create a new heaven and a new earth are called "my servants." They will live in the idyllic conditions set out in verses 19-25, compared with the punishment described in verses 7, 12, 13-15 for those who have rejected YHWH.

The issue we raise is whether the servants are those who are faithful, but who may or may not be of Israelite descent. This statement can be challenged by verses 8-9 that declare that the descendants of Jacob and Judah will inherit Jerusalem. The crux is in the last line of verse 10 with its statement "for those who have sought me out." If we are prepared to consider Isaiah 56–66 as a single piece of literature, then Isaiah 65 must be considered in light of what was declared in Isaiah 63:7–64:11 and in the earlier chapters. In the lament, the message is quite explicit; Israel did not seek out their God. Their pleading words seem to recognize their sin, and they have a dawning realization that perhaps this time God will not respond to them. If that

[7] According to one theory, the chapter is divided into three sections, verses 1-7, 8-12, and 13-25 (Fohrer, Elliger, Steck) or verses 1-7, 8-16, and 17-25 (E. C. Webster). Within this composition, verses 8-16 can be broken into two subsections, 8-12 and 13-16. A second proposal, K. Koenen, "Textkritische Anmerkungen zu schwierigen Stellen im Tritojesajabuch," has verses 16b-24 written first, followed by verses 8-16a, with glosses appearing in 15ab, 16, and 25, verses 1-7 are complete in themselves with Koenen treating verses 1-16 as a unit, 564–73. To deal with the chapter as a literary unit without any divisions has some appeal when we see the complex redactional activity suggested in recent articles and monographs.

is the case, the servants will be a different group of people from those in the lament. Who are the people who have sought YHWH? We assume there will be some Israelites who have remained faithful and perhaps also the foreigners and eunuchs mentioned in Isaiah 56:1-8 who are called servants.

We can only hope to argue the above position if we are able to show a strong possibility that Isaiah 56–66 was deliberately put together to be read as a whole. Beuken maintains that this is quite feasible. His proposal takes the theme of "servants" and suggests that it has been carried through from Isaiah 56.[8] Besides Beuken's suggestion there are other themes which appear to carry through from Isaiah 56, such as references to the chosen, a strong theme of righteousness, and the announcement in 56:8 that God will gather yet others. In Isaiah 57 and 58 we can see already the separation between those who will be punished because they are accused of many sins (57:1-13) and those who will find peace because they have a humble and contrite heart (57:14-21). Other parallels between Isaiah 65 and Isaiah 57/58 are: a similar list of cultic sins even to the garden being a place of evil; references to the people forgetting God (57:11); and the positive assertion that the people will call (58:9). Isaiah 57:1-13 appears to have a comparable literary structure to Isaiah 65:1-7. These similarities would support the possibility that Isaiah 56–66 has been created at the one time.

If we take seriously the close connections between Isaiah 65 and the lament in Isaiah 63:7–64:11, then it reinforces further the argument for a deliberate structure across not just these chapters but the whole of Isaiah 56–66. Some people, as we have indicated, argue that Isaiah 65 was a piece of literature composed of disparate parts (Whybray, Pauritsch, and others). From our discussion the whole chapter seems to be very tightly structured, both in its theological content and the literary flow. Verses 1-12 lead into the announcement about the servants in verses 13-25 and a description of the new creation. In addition, the theological issue of God calling and the failure of the people to respond is present in verses 1, 12, and 24.

[8] W.A.M. Beuken, "The Main Themes of Trito-Isaiah," 67–87.

Furthermore, the number of common phrases is significant and cannot be viewed simply as a coincidence. Isaiah 65:1-2 both answers and denies the complaints of the people in 63:10-11, 15, 17, 19b; 64:4, 7. The people realize that God is angry (64:5), which is verified in 65:5b. Their complaint of God's silence in 64:11b is answered in 65:6. By their own admission they have sinned (64:5, 6a, 8), and their punishment is stated in 65:7, 12, 13-15. Israel asks YHWH to return for "his servants' sake" in 63:17. When YHWH does answer, the nation of Israel can no longer regard itself as YHWH's servant—only those people who have been faithful. We assert that the connections mentioned above confirm the concept of a deliberate construction of Isaiah 63:7 to 65:25, which may indeed extend to Isaiah 66:24. In addition, the proclamation in Isaiah 65 makes explicit the issues raised in Isaiah 57:13b, 15b; 58:13-14 and therefore reinforces the possibility of Isaiah 56–66 as the creation of one person.

Before we point to a number of other connections within Isaiah 65 in table II (Appendix), we shall include a brief comment on what constitutes a connection. Elliger and Odeberg use a word comparison, and Hanson looks at literary style and theological concepts. Zimmerli has three levels of connection: direct citations, freer imitations, and more remote reminiscences.[9] We maintain that a "connection" to be justified has to include an examination of both the original and the new context of the suggested phrase or idea. For example, to be an exact parallel the proposed text has to agree in words, theological issues, and address the same faith group (not necessarily the same generation). What we have found in many instances in Isaiah 56–66 is the reapplication of an idea to a new situation. Many scholars use the past context of a particular word or saying to interpret it with the same meaning in the new setting. We believe it is important not only to examine the past context of a particular phrase but also to be aware that it can have a different meaning in a new setting. Literary genre should never be tied to a past framework. Indeed, most, if not all, suggested "connections" have a different theological intention in their

---

[9] W. Zimmerli, "Zur Sprache Tritojesajas," 217–33.

new setting, but one can see this only by an examination of both contexts.

Our assertion about the close connections between Isaiah 65 and the lament in Isaiah 63:7–64:11 would deny the suggestion by Tomasino that Isaiah 65 and 66:22-24 were a later insertion.[10] In addition, there are analogies to chapter 66 that suggest Isaiah 65 had to be part of an original structure, beginning at the lament and continuing to the end of Isaiah 66 (65:1-5//66:3-4, 17 have a similar message of apostasy, 65:12b//66:4; 65:18-19//66:10, 14). Clearly, Isaiah 65 is a response to the lament that makes it inconceivable that it was inserted into Isaiah 56–66 at a later time.

We discern also two further examples of "an oxymoron." One is the ironic statement in 65:5 which could refer to the behavior of the priests (Ezek 44:19), and the other is the new definition of "servant" (Isa 65:15). These statements serve to confront the orthodox position with a radical theological message that turns upside down people's usual perspective about themselves. By the time we get to Isaiah 65, the message is so open and angry against the apostate Israelites that the necessity to use such literary methods has decreased. Their sinful behavior reads as though it is a present experience that is an open and established reality. In light of the evidence, we propose that Isaiah 65 is a carefully structured piece of literature that enhances the theological proclamation contained within it.

The structure and theological concepts employed by Trito-Isaiah in Isaiah 65 proclaim a message of acceptance, hope, and joy to a group of people named "my chosen." YHWH's frustration and impatience with Israel results in an offer of new life to those who are faithful. God names the new community and creates a new Jerusalem. The people of Israel who assumed they were the "servants" and "chosen" of YHWH have been displaced by a new group of people who remained faithful and are able to call on YHWH. It is a powerful message and one that surely would cause friction among those who believed themselves to be YHWH's chosen people. If Isaiah 56–66 is a rebuttal

---

[10] A. J. Tomasino, "Isaiah 1:1–2:4 and 63–66 . . .," thinks that Isaiah 66:1 follows on better to 64:11 and Isaiah 65 contains less direct links to Isaiah 1, 96.

of the powerful priestly group's policies, the writer would have struggled to present his case which was in opposition to the Torah. Trito-Isaiah had to justify his argument for the inclusion of foreigners on the basis of the faith. Indeed, the ones who are acceptable to God are those who have remained faithful and humble.

Isaiah 66:1-16 has a pattern in which the message begins with the initial announcement of God who states what priority he seeks in his people (vv. 1-2). After this initial announcement alternate sections speak of the rewards for those who hear God and the punishment of those who fail to hear God and hate their brethren. This pattern can also be discerned in verses 17-24. Thus, verses 3-4, 5b, 6b, 14b-17, 24 speak about the punishment for the apostate ones and 2b, 5a, 7-14a, 18-23 speak about the reward for the faithful ones. This pattern suggests that Isaiah 66 is a literary unit. In addition, the close structuring of judgment/salvation oracles in this chapter reinforces the theological message.[11]

In table III (Appendix) the links between Isaiah 65 and 66 are summarized. In addition, the pattern of Isaiah 65 is similar to Isaiah 66. That is, God speaks initially, stating an aspect of his nature (v. 1), the apostasy of those who are unfaithful is detailed in verses 2-7, then the division between the faithful and unfaithful is described in verses 8-16, followed by the reward for the faithful (vv. 17-25). Besides a parallel literary pattern, there are also similar issues in each chapter, especially the denunciation of those who commit apostasy. We note the sections which are particularly close in thought: 66:3-4//65:11-12; 66:4 //65:11; 66:10//65:18-19. In 66:12-14//65:19-25 different images are used, but they depict parallel ideas of the ideal Jerusalem. We observed the connections both in content and style

---

[11] Hanson, *The Dawn of Apocalyptic,* says Trito-Isaiah combines within one oracle the judgment only oracles of Isaiah 1–39 with the oracles of promise in Isaiah 40–55, 145, 171. R. Rendtorff, *The Old Testament: An Introduction,* supports Hanson's position on the possibility of a new genre, "Now judgement and salvation belong indissolubly together and are related to each other," 200. In addition, this new literary genre is present in other post-exilic writings besides Isaiah 56–66 (Ezekiel, Jeremiah).

with Isaiah 65 and agree with many scholars that these chapters were constructed at the same time.

Isaiah 66 begins by putting YHWH firmly at the center of all creation, both the physical and the spiritual. Human beings have limited creative powers that cannot be compared with those of God. Those people who believe that the Temple is of crucial importance and the center of worship are being told there are other priorities, at least in the eyes of God. This message surely would have disturbed those such as Ezekiel who set a priority on the temple and worship practice. Verse 2b states clearly that God is seeking a person who is "humble and contrite in spirit, and trembles at my word." We noted this same phrase in Isaiah 57. The right attitude to God takes precedence over sacrificial offerings, especially sacrificial methods which contravene the Torah.

To summarize the discussion, Isaiah 66:1-4 is a cohesive unit that decisively incorporates themes from the previous chapter —sacrificial sins, inability to listen, refusal to respond to YHWH's call. The verses have a twofold purpose. On the one hand, they reinforce the condemnation of the unfaithful and apostate Israelites and, on the other hand, they uphold and define those to whom YHWH will relate (v. 2b). Verse 1 neither rejects temple worship in general nor the specific act of worship in the Jerusalem Temple. Rather, the focus of the verses reiterates the power and control of God over all the creation and condemns wrong sacrificial practices. Undoubtedly, the condemnation persists because the people have failed to answer the call of God and have continued in their own evil ways.

Apparently those who follow in God's way are the focus of hatred from a group within their own community. What may have been intended as a sarcastic comment by these "brethren" (v. 5b) becomes a reality when the description of God's new creation is described in verses 7-14a. Very powerful images of birth and suckling are used to portray the nurture and care provided by Jerusalem and YHWH. God is a mother who gives comfort. The recipients of God's care are described in verse 2a and again in verse 5a. In order to press the point home, verse 14b ensures the reader knows that God's hand is with the servants, but his anger is still against his enemies. The identity of the "enemies" has caused much speculation. We argue that when verses 5-6 are read together, the "enemies" are the ones who hate the servants. Various suggestions for the identity of the enemy have been proposed which include: the Zadokite priests (Achtemeier, Hanson), the landholders in the north (Scullion), the ones who have returned to Jerusalem (Pauritsch), the unfaithful (Beuken), and the nations (Steck). Conversely, the identity of the righteous could be: the Levitical prophetic party (Achtemeier), the visionary group (Hanson), the first return group of exiles (Pauritsch), and a group who comprised those left in the land together with some returned Israelites who were sympathetic to the inclusion of foreigners. On the basis of the experience of those left in the land, we suggest they were willing to accept foreigners into the community both in marriage and worship. The need for the exilic community to retain their identity as Israelites suggests a closed community that held closely to the Torah requirements. We witness this attitude in the writings of Ezra/Nehemiah and Ezekiel. Therefore, the writings of Isaiah 56–66 appear to support those who have an inclusive attitude against those who are dominant in the Temple. Verse 14b with its reference to servants recalls Isaiah 65 in which the servants are the faithful ones as opposed to the enemies.

One unusual saying "trembles at my word" is particular to Isaiah 66 and Ezra 9:4, 10:3, which may imply the same historical date for both texts. Apart from the descriptions of explicit condemnation, which have reminders of Ezekiel 8, 44, there are few other indicators for dating Isaiah 66:1-17.

Four examples of an "oxymoron" are found in Isaiah 66:1-17. In each case the particular theological reference that in the past had applied only to the Israelites is now given to the newly defined group of "faithful." In verses 7-12 those who have heard God's call will experience the birth and ongoing nurture of Jerusalem and those Israelites who have refused to hear YHWH's call may be excluded. The idea of Jerusalem nurturing anyone other than the Israelite nation was unthinkable, and yet Trito-Isaiah dared to suggest this to a community, which would have been horrified by this prospect. His message in verse 13 which stated that a woman could bring comfort caused most people to find a substitute translation; although, it may have been an expansion of the idea in Jeremiah 31:22b. Finally the divine warrior image of God in verses 15-16 has demonstrated in the past that God was on the side of the Israelites because God's anger was against the nations and Israel's enemies. We believe that in the context of Isaiah 66 the enemies are the unfaithful Israelites themselves. Each time Trito-Isaiah employs an "oxymoron," he confronts the Israelites to rethink their attitude to God and redefines the community to whom God will relate.

Isaiah 66:18-24 paints a picture of an all-powerful God who knows everything and chooses to gather people from every race and tongue to see the revelation of his glory. This glory of the Lord appears and functions in different ways. In Isaiah 66 God uses foreign nations as agents of his glory. Whereas in Isaiah 60–62 the glory rests upon Zion, in Ezekiel the "glory" is synonymous with the theophany itself (1:28). The one constant is the knowledge that "glory" is another way of saying God is present. It appears that God's glory is free to move when and where the Lord dictates (Ezek 8–11), so people may never try to dictate the presence or movement of God's glory. In Ezekiel 40–48 the glory moves back to the rebuilt Temple, indicating that God's presence has returned to be with his people.

In Isaiah 66:21 the glory of God will be declared to other nations (Tarshish, Put, *et al*) by the survivors of the nations. This action confronts Ezekiel's harsh indictment of the foreigner's status within the Temple. Surely God must approve of the nations if they are able to see his glory (v. 18) and declare it to others (v. 19). And even more radically, God takes some of them to be priests and Levites. This is an exceptional proclamation, in view of the legal prohibitions against the inclusion of foreigners in the Torah and the book of Ezekiel. Following the argument above, verse 21 (and even from *them*) refers to the nations. Therefore some people from the nations will become priests and Levites. This is a radical and provocative idea.[12]

---

[12] D. H. Odendaal, "The Eschatological Expectation of Isaiah 40–66 with Special Reference to Israel and the Nations." A connection has been proposed by Odendaal between Isaiah 61:6 and 66:21. In Isaiah 61:6 the *Israelites*

The third person plural pronominal suffix הם (them) acts as a connection in verses 18-21. The same subject (nations and tongues) flows from verse 18 and connects both verses 20 and 21 with the suffix הם. The use of גם (even/also) reinforces the unusual interpretation of verse 21 as it normally introduces a new thing, "even from them, I will take. . . ." The Qumran scroll gives a further emphasis with the inclusion of לי (to me), which leaves no doubt about the identity of whom they will serve.[13]

However, some scholars switch the subject in verse 21 from the Israelites, who will be brought back by the survivors of the nations in verse 20, proposing that "some of them" in verse 21 now refers to the nations.[14] This position supports Westermann's argument for verse 20 as a later insertion. Those who have a change of subject from verse 20 (Israelites) to verse 21 (nations), and who do not embrace Westermann's position, argue that we need to assess the intent of the verse within the overall context and conclude that the foreigners will become priests and Levites. If that is the case, why do they not interpret "your brethren" in verse 20 as the brothers of the foreign survivors? It is inconsistent to use the context for supporting the idea of "nations" in verse 21 and then deny the same argument for "your brethren" in verse 20. We agree with Koenen on the universal and radical character of these verses.

---

will become priests and ministers and the *aliens* will be servants. Despite the unambiguous message of Isaiah 61:6, it has been used by Odendaal to support an interpretation of Isaiah 66:21 in which the priests and Levites will be chosen from the foreign nations. While rejecting Odendaal's argument, we accept that priests and Levites will be chosen from the nations for the following reasons, 186.

[13] 1QIsa, Plate LIV.

[14] Achtemeier, *The Community and Message of Isaiah 56–66*, 21. F. Delitzsch, *Biblical Commentary on the Prophecies of Isaiah*, 513. G.A.F. Knight, *The New Israel*, 117. Muilenburg, "Isaiah Chapters 40–66," 772. Westermann, *Isaiah 40–66*, 426. Whybray, *Isaiah 40–66*, 291. D. R. Jones, *Isaiah 56–66 and Joel*, does not want to accept that verse 21 refers to the Gentiles, although the context may demand it, 21.

Some, like Schramm take an opposite view and identify the Israelites as the subject of verse 21 which means they become priests and Levites.[15]

We accept the Masoretic Text and the interpretation of separate cultic offices, Levites and priests.[16] Achtemeier, on the other hand, maintains that there is only one office of Levitical priests (not priests and Levites, as in the RSV).[17] However, if the author had intended to designate one office he would have rendered the Hebrew, לכהנים (Levitical priests). Achtemeier bases her argument on a conflict she perceives within the text between the Zadokite priests and the Levites who had been excluded in Ezekiel's ideal community (40–48), but it is difficult to confirm with our lack of historical sources. For her, Isaiah 56–66 depicts the culmination of a long struggle between these cultic groups and in particular represents the Levitical-reform-Deuteronomic-prophetic-group. The Hebrew text lacks support for her argument by naming two cultic groups in Isaiah 66:21.

Verses 18-21 proclaim radical ideas which may be in their embryonic form in other books of the Hebrew Scriptures, especially in Deutero-Isaiah that many perceive as the epitome of universalism.[18] On the other hand, Isaiah 56:1-8 has similar

---

[15] B. Schramm, *The Opponents of Third Isaiah,* 172.

[16] Delitzsch, *Biblical Commentary . . .,* 514. H. J. Kraus, "Das Evangelium der unbekannten Propheten 40–66," notes two textual emendations, (a) the added "ו" which is not in the MT, denotes the separation into two priestly classes; (b) the "ל" is dropped from "ללוים" in some Greek MSS and Targums (BHS), 254. Koenen, "Textkritische Anmerkungen . . .," note 15 has great detail on this issue of Levites and priests. Deuteronomy is the model behind verse 21, which has "Levitical priests" not the two separate classes. In the context of the fifth century, which seems a reasonable time for the redaction of these verses, the two classes of priesthood are attested to in the Priestly material. There is insufficient evidence to suggest only the one group. Targum Isaiah retains "priests and Levites," B. D. Chilton, *The Isaiah Targum,* 128.

[17] Achtemeier, *The Community and Message of Isaiah 56–66,* 17. The literal translation of the Hebrew is "for priests, for Levites" with some manuscripts adding "and." BHS, 779. Whybray, *Isaiah 40–66,* 292.

[18] Hanson, *The Dawn of Apocalyptic,* perceives close connections between Isaiah 66:18-24 and Zechariah 14:14-21 because they have the same

inclusive views about foreigners/nations as Isaiah 66:18-24, which is why so many scholars claim them as "bookends" for Isaiah 56–66.

The various positions on "the sending out and gathering in of the nations" in Isaiah 66:18-21 can be summarized as:

1. God will gather the nations by setting a sign among them. From those who respond to the sign will be sent out "survivors" to the farther nations who have not heard of God's glory. These people will bring in other foreign nations to Jerusalem, some of whom will become priests and Levites (Grant-Henderson).

2. God will gather the nations by setting a sign among them. Those who respond to the sign will be sent out to the farther nations who have not heard of God's glory. These foreigners will bring in the remainder of the Israelite people still in the far countries and some of the Israelites will become priests and Levites (Davies, Schramm, Whybray).

3. God will gather the nations by setting a sign among them. Those who respond to the sign will be sent out to the farther nations who have not heard of God's glory. Foreigners are sent out to bring in the Israelites and some of the foreigners become priests and Levites (Achtemeier, Delitzsch, Jones, Knight, Odendaal, Westermann).

4. "Your brethren" in verse 20 could include both Israelites and foreigners, which means the priests and Levites in verse 21 are both Israelites and foreigners (Beuken).

Acceptance of position 1, for which we have argued, means that Isaiah 66:18-21 becomes the final high point of Isaiah 56–66. It gathers up all the previous arguments and proclamations from Isaiah 56:1-8 through the next eleven chapters to culminate in an extraordinary vision of an inclusive commu-

---

indifference to history and a parallel universalism, which we refute after an examination of the texts. The first reason could apply to a very large segment of the Bible and is not unique to Isaiah and Zechariah, 388–89.

nity. This position also implies connections between Isaiah 66:18-21 and 56:1-8, and indeed, both passages speak of God gathering in non-Israelites. In 56:8 God declares his purposes in relation to foreigners and the declaration in 66:18 is to the nations. A second link is the destination of the Holy Mountain for the foreigners and nations (56:7; 66:20).

In approaching verses 22-24 we note the different ways in which scholars have interpreted the text. Either it is perceived as a literal happening or as an acted parable of a future state. In the analysis of poetry and prose there are times when a truth is stated which ought not to be pulled apart, line by line, as literal truth, but allowed to speak to us as a whole. The difficulty arises in verse 23 when some people try to make literal sense of how "all flesh" could worship each week. In this situation the character of the images dictates an interpretation that contains the truth without the need to be pedantic about the actual practice. Therefore, we interpret verse 23 in this sense: that all people will be able to worship YHWH without any impediment. The imagery in verse 22 emphasizes both the new event referred to in verses 18-21 and the eternal nature of the promise about the descendants (22b).

Prophetic writing reports experiences which occur within the life of the community and proclaims their significance under God. An example of this is Isaiah 40–55; it discusses the return to Zion as a future event which becomes a reality. The prose of verse 24 describes a future judgment in graphic terms as a warning to a group of people who are committing apostasy in the life of the community. Its reality seems consistent with the historical evidence about the valley of Hinnom outside Jerusalem.

We note that verse 24 does not have a closing formula that is present in the previous verse. Both the dire judgments in Isaiah 65:3b-5 and 66:17 end with the closing formula "thus says the Lord." This is surprising, for it would both round off the book and give authority to the words of warning. The omission of the formula supports the arguments of those scholars who see this verse as a much later addition.

In the following summary we highlight the major themes and issues relating to Isaiah 66:17-24. The absence of verbs and the possible controversial subject matter cause great difficulty in discerning the proclamation contained within it. As we study these eight verses, we observe the severity of the judgment contained in the enclosing verses 17 and 24. The judgment is addressed to those who commit particularly flagrant cultic sins and the judgment is equally harsh in both verses. Within the proclamation of judgment is an announcement of God's purposes. We take seriously the context on which to base our argument about the role and status of the nations.

There are several places where the text is ambiguous: for example, the identity of "survivors" in verse 19, "your brethren" in verse 20, "some of them" in verse 21, "your descendants" in verse 22. In each of the above examples, the scholar's interpretation depends on whether Israelites or nations (v. 19 survivors) go to the nations and bring back Israelites or foreigners (v. 20 your brethren). The same difficulty occurs in verse 21 and verse 22. We have chosen to remain with the message as dictated by the context of verse 18 and conclude that verses 18-24 refer to the nations and the role they play in Israel's future.

The phrase "says the Lord" both reinforces and gives authority to the message, especially when it is used five times in seven verses (vv. 17-23). The implication must be that the message is exceptional if it needs the frequent use of this phrase. It is a literary construction that supports our interpretation of the passage.

The historical milieu for Isaiah 66:17-24 is very hard to discern. The fact that the named nations in verse 19 are also mentioned in Ezekiel 27 does not give a firm dating. The reference to the priests and Levites indicates the Temple is functioning and could connect this passage with Ezekiel 40–48. We observed that the particular term "YHWH seba'ot" is missing in Ezekiel and Trito-Isaiah, although present in many other prophetic writings (Isaiah 1–39, MT Jeremiah, Haggai, Zechariah 1–8, Malachi).[19] Consequently, we are left with uncertainty when we try and compare Isaiah 66:17-24 with other texts in the Hebrew Scriptures.

---

[19] C. T. Begg, "The Absence of YHWH seba'ot in Isaiah 56-66," 7.

We might find it more useful to see what sort of situation is implied by the message within the verses. Verse 17 indicates a period in which a community has abused the cultic laws and the consequent punishment is particularly severe (v. 24). A great fear lurks behind the severity of the punishment in this verse. Perhaps the apostasy is so bad that the people are in danger of losing the Yahwistic faith to syncretistic worship. Notwithstanding, in Isaiah 66:17-24, along with the punishment, is the promise of everlasting lineage and universal worship. Indeed, God will have foreigners as priests and Levites. In summary, verses 17-24 contain dire punishment and unconditional promises of God's purposes.

Nehemiah and Ezekiel are concerned also about purity of worship. They see the answer in the exclusion of foreigners from the life and worship of Israel. The message of Isaiah 56–66 would have been anathema to these writers. This is not only because of the announcement of an inclusive community but also because of the recruitment of priests and Levites from the nations to serve the Lord.

We observed earlier that many scholars believe Isaiah 66:17-24 and Isaiah 56:1-8 were attached at the same time to make bookends for the remaining chapters 56–66. The similarities are based largely on the inclusive nature of both sections in which the foreigners and nations are accepted as part of the community of Israel and even become priests and Levites. A significant difference occurs in the terminology whereby Isaiah 56:1-8 refers only to *foreigners* and 66:17-24 refers only to the *nations*.

Other similarities, besides its inclusive nature, include the use of the verb קבץ (to gather together) with its new focus on gathering peoples other than the Israelites. In both sections the people will come to a house of prayer/house of the Lord on my holy mountain. A major difference between the texts is the agent who is instrumental for the return of the nations or foreigners. In Isaiah 56:1-8, God is the one who will act in order for the new things to occur (56:5, 7, 8). In Isaiah 66:18-24, God acts initially in gathering the nations and then directs them to be his agents, enabling his purposes to come to fruition.

An examination of the texts in question (Isa 56:1-8 and 66:17-24) fails to give overwhelming evidence for the close similarity that some scholars claim. In view of the exploration above, 66:18-24 could be subsequent to 56:1-8 and thus address a later situation. No one has queried the different literary styles of the two sections: poetry (Isa 56:1-8) and prose (66:18-24), different use of words for non-Israelite people (foreigners and nations), different agent for the return of the outcasts, different names for the Temple (although partially similar). Both passages mention the Sabbath, but there is no express exhortation to the people in Isaiah 66:17-24 to keep the Sabbath, as there is in Isaiah 56:1-8.

Isaiah 56:8 could be continued in 66:18-24, which shows how God will gather the scattered ones and the method by which God will do it. Further connections are noted with the material in chapters 65–66 (66:17//65:3-5; 66:22//65:17). If there is a deliberate construction of chapters 65–66 (63:7–66:24), we may not speak solely of Isaiah 66:17-24 as a bookend joined onto Isaiah 66:16. The close interweaving of ideas and language encourages us to consider a single creative author for Isaiah 56–66. In conclusion, we disagree with those who regard 56:1-8 and 66:18-24 as bookends for chapters 56:9–66:17.

As a result of studying Isaiah 56:1-8 and 66:17-24, we have questioned the strong tradition that accepts them as bookends to Isaiah 56–66. The differences mentioned above fail to be included in scholars' discussions of this material. Although we disagree with their designation as bookends, we tentatively suggest another form of relationship that is different from most other scholars. If, as we believe, Isaiah 56–66 was written at one time, 66:17-24 is the culmination of a message that has unfolded through all eleven chapters. Isaiah 56:1-8 is the prologue that culminates in 66:17-24 rather than bookends added to material already compiled.

At this point we look again at possible historical situations for Isaiah 56–66. We noted that scholars are almost unanimous in their agreed dating on Isaiah 60–62. No such unanimity exists for the creation of Isaiah 56–66 in response to some threatening situation. One of the most likely periods for consideration is the time of Ezekiel and Nehemiah. Both of these writings strongly condemn association with foreigners. Ezekiel excludes them from the Temple (Ezek 44:4-14) and Nehemiah from joining in marriage with Israelites (Neh 13:23-30). Nehemiah reads as though marriages have occurred—"I contended with them and cursed them and beat some of them and pulled out their hair" (v. 25)—and he continues in the same vein, making the Israelites promise that they will not give their sons and daughters in marriage to people from Ashdod, Ammon, and Moab. Ezekiel implies that foreigners have already been admitted into the sanctuary (44:6-7) and his pronouncement is against this practice. Any foreigners who were involved in the temple service or married to an Israelite were in danger of exclusion because of the words of Nehemiah and Ezekiel.

Both Ezekiel and Nehemiah demonstrate a reality that foreigners were a part of the Israelite community. Their pronouncements read as a reaction to the foreigners' participation and involvement in the life of Israel. We submit that Isaiah 56–66 is part of a considered apologetic on behalf of a group of people who accepts and includes foreigners within their community. They are a group that not only contends with the strong words of Ezekiel and Nehemiah, but also has the Torah against them (Lev 26:14-45; Deut 23:1-8). Nevertheless, their writings have been allowed to remain as part of the Scriptures. It is this practice, which allows passages with conflicting views to remain in the Scriptures, that we address next.

It has been noted by Seitz that

> there is significant evidence that the book's editors often carefully preserved the integrity of the tradition that preceded them. Thus, to some extent, the perspective of the earlier material resisted the reconceptualization of their role in the redactional additions. Rather than subsuming or reorganizing the materials into their new redactional conception of the whole, the editors allowed the early materials to stand over against the perspective implicit in their redactional additions.[20]

He makes this statement in reference to the whole book of Isaiah that was formed through a gradual redactional process.

---

[20] C. R. Seitz, "Isaiah 1–66: Making sense of the whole," 107–9.

We suggest his ideas apply also to Isaiah 56–66 as the work of one author. When 56–66 is read as a piece of literature in its entirety, we are confronted with the contrary positions discussed above. What message about the foreigners are we expected to hear when the inclusive proclamations of Isaiah 56:1-8 and 66:17-24 surround the deferential proclamations in 60–62? A general understanding of the growth of the Hebrew Scriptures adopted by scholars is to take the latest additions as the corrective to what was previously regarded as the norm. In this case the role of the nations defined in Isaiah 60–62 was part of the earlier material written soon after the return of the exiles. When this material is picked up and used by Trito-Isaiah together with Isaiah 56:1-8 and 66:17-24, the status and role of the nations are changed and the reader is expected to read the eleven chapters in their total context. Furthermore, I propose that Isaiah 56:1-8 introduces a block of material (Isaiah 56–66) that contains a decisive shift in the prophetic message by giving it divine authorization. An examination of the Qumran scroll of Isaiah confirms that the radical messages in Isaiah 56 and 66 have been allowed to remain without any modifications by the later scribes of the Qumran material.

Scripture contains many different forms of literature that are structured to present an argument for a particular position. Paul in the Christian Scriptures first presents one side of an argument and then proceeds to demolish it: for example, Galatians 5:16-26 overturns the argument in Galatians 5:1-15, so we are left in no doubt what our response is meant to be. In some Hebrew Scriptures we have the same form as appears in Isaiah 56–66 where contrary positions about an issue are allowed to stand side by side or even deliberately created in this manner: for example, the account in the Deuteronomic History of the monarchy's beginnings in Israel (1 Sam 8–12). We are expected to take a position on the issue. Thus Isaiah 60–62 speaks of an attitude to the foreigners that was prevalent at one time in Israel's history, but the advent of Isaiah 56:1-8 and 66:18-24 presents a new and radically different attitude to foreigners and nations.

Why keep the earlier material or deliberately choose to construct a piece of writing with opposing views in juxtaposition?[21] By retaining both positions we perceive more clearly the shift in theological understanding about the nations in Isaiah 56–66. Trito-Isaiah's position is given when he encloses Isaiah 60–62 with the proclamation about the status and role of foreigners and nations in Isaiah 56:1-8 and 66:17-24. His intention is to show how one position is required by God rather than the other. This is achieved by the divine authority given when the emphatic voice of God speaks in the first-person singular and by the phrase "thus says the Lord." Moreover, the message offers new promises for the reconstituted community. As Smith says:

> The author takes up a number of these terms and themes from 60:1–63:6 in order to clarify, or possibly correct, the statements made by TI [Trito-Isaiah] about the place of the foreign prose-lytes in the new community, and at the same time to reassure proselytes in the new community, whose anxieties had been aroused by the proclamation of TI, that they were not going to be relegated to this second class citizenship.[22]

Trito-Isaiah stands in a tradition which has allowed texts with diverse proclamations to be alongside one another. We believe it has been part of the author's deliberate construction of chapters 56–66.

We have endeavored to show that 56–66 was created as one piece of literature with a deliberate use of contradictory messages in order to challenge the strong messages of Ezra/Nehemiah and Ezekiel (the particular texts will be examined in chapter 5). In particular, we made the specific claim that Isaiah 56:1-8 acts as a prologue, foreshadowing the proclamation of Isaiah 56:9–66:24. The identity of the group in the prologue that includes the righteous, the foreigners, and the eunuchs is all part of the same group spoken of in Isaiah 65 and 66. The group

---

[21] D. Carr, "Reaching for Unity in Isaiah,"argues against scholars who try to find a unity in Isaiah 1–66 which smooths out the book and denies the plurality of texts within the book. He certainly points us to the danger of imposing an unitary literary shape on the final form. However, he fails to suggest reasons for authors or redactors leaving or creating their works with contrary views standing side by side in the text, 79–80.

[22] P. A. Smith, *Rhetoric and Redaction in Trito-Isaiah*, 59.

is feeling threatened and is facing expulsion from the community and condemnation. Furthermore, this group is facing expulsion from the Temple, and many of them are required to give up spouses and their children if they have married foreigners.

Pauritsch, Scullion, and Orlinsky believe the faithful ones are a group who came from Babylon seeking to belong to the Jerusalem congregation.[23] On the other hand, we favor the notion of a group who were descendants of those who had stayed in the land. Whichever it is, there is no doubt about the call to be included and the judgment on those who are unfaithful.

The identity of the people late in the fifth century who fostered the different views mentioned above still causes much debate among scholars. We shall discuss their suggestions in chapter 5. Scholars have considered the possible identity of the groups or endeavored to see the genesis of groups such as the Pharisees, Samaritans, and Jews in the above texts (Ezekiel, Ezra/Nehemiah, Isaiah 56–66). One of the most recent studies has opposed Hanson's thesis, which states that 56–66 was the written protest of a visionary group of Deutero-Isaianic disciples.[24] Instead of portraying an opposition group, Schramm views the oracles as parallel to those in Ezekiel expressing the same concern: that is, the cultic apostasy of the people of Israel.

We both agree and disagree with Schramm. We agree that Trito-Isaiah and Ezekiel have the same concern, but as noted above we differ on the way each book addresses the issues. We concur that the opposition is not a visionary party led by Deutero-Isaianic disciples but disagree that Trito-Isaiah is one of the same group as Ezekiel and Ezra. Isaiah 56–66 with its inclusive proclamation about the foreigner and eunuch contradicts the Torah. Further, 56–66 fails to condemn mixed marriages as is the case in Nehemiah. While the idea of parties is unacceptable, we accept that a group of people in 56–66 are struggling to be included within a community that is intent on

---

[23] Pauritsch, *Die Neue Gemeinde*, 246–50. Scullion, "Studies in Isaiah cc. 56–66," 157. H. M. Orlinsky, "Nationalism-Universalism and Internationalism in Ancient Israel," 220.

[24] Schramm, *The Opponents of Third Isaiah*, 85.

excluding them. This latter position is observed in Ezra, Nehemiah, and Ezekiel. Barker believes the group has someone (Trito-Isaiah) writing on their behalf, who is very strong in his condemnation of those who have not listened to God and followed the covenant.[25] No direct evidence is available to support Barker's suggestion.

Trito-Isaiah had to call on all his literary skill in order to confront the theology of Ezekiel and Ezra/Nehemiah and to get his message heard. One of the techniques that he employed was what we have called "an oxymoron" because it reversed an understanding that the Israelite people had of their relationship with God. Our exegesis of the passages yielded examples of this literary method. In table IV (Appendix) we are able to see a number of theological phrases used by Ezekiel, Ezra/Nehemiah, and Trito-Isaiah. For example, in Nehemiah and Ezra the foreigners are to be separate from the Israelites. On the other hand, the foreigners in Isaiah 56:3 will not be allowed to say they are separate from the Lord's people. The new community

---

[25] M. Barker, *The Older Testament,* proposes that Trito-Isaiah writes on behalf of the "people of the land," that is, the ones who remained in Jerusalem in 598 and 587 B.C.E. These people are excluded now by those exiles who have returned and taken over the management of the Temple and city, supported by money from the Persians, 192. Whether Trito-Isaiah is a returnee exile sympathetic to the "people of the land" or one of those who remained in the land is unclear from Barker's writings. Although Barker identifies the "people of the land" as the people left in the land, other scholars have differing opinions. For example, E. W. Nicholson, "The Meaning of the Expression 'am haʾares' in the Old Testament," notes the indeterminate and various meanings of this term and stresses that the concrete sense must be read from the context and the historical situation, 59–66. J. Weinberg, *The Citizen-Temple Community,* applies this principle when he gives the term two different interpretations depending on the context in the sixth to fifth centuries. The "am haʾares" is both the self-designation of the emerging citizen-temple community and a designation for opposite socio-political structures (Samaritans). In Ezra the "am ha'ares" refers to the enemies of the community and in Haggai/Zechariah it is a self-designated term. Later still it became a pejorative term, 67–74. It is apparent from this very brief comment how difficult it is to define the term "am haʾares."

is referred to as God's "chosen," "servants," "they will be blessed," all terms which referred initially to the Israelite nation. The definition now excludes Israelites who may be unfaithful but includes those who are "humble and contrite of heart." The literary tool that we refer to as "an oxymoron" challenges the audience to hear a message that would have been directly opposed to those proclamations of Ezra/Nehemiah and Ezekiel.[26]

The other literary method employed by Trito-Isaiah to foster his message was an oracle which included within it both judgment and promise. By putting both messages in close proximity, the proclamation of judgment on the unfaithful and reward to the faithful were reinforced.

The above proposals about an inclusive proclamation can only be appreciated when Isaiah 56–66 is read as a unit. We turn now to the suggestions which could support such a reading. The first indicator is the presence of "salvation-judgment" oracles in chapters throughout Isaiah 56–66. Examples of the "salvation-judgment oracle that came to characterize the postexilic period" are in Isaiah 57, 58, 59, 65, and 66.[27] We are aware this form is absent in Isaiah 60–62 and have explained it as part of the author's intention to use material on occasions without changing it. The presence of this unusual new genre lends support to the possibility of a single authorship for Isaiah 56–66.

Our argument for a single author is prompted by the close links within the text of Isaiah 56–66 which are demonstrated in table V (Appendix). For example, 56:1-8 acts as a prologue that begins by stating what is important to God in relationship. Justice and righteousness are exhorted by God which is followed

---

[26] K. Dell, "The Misuse of Forms in Amos," 45–61. Dell uses a different term to describe a similar process. She says that Amos deliberately misuses forms in order to emphasize the newness of the message. The changed form is employed in a radically new way and in a radically new context. The process we call "an oxymoron" achieves the same purpose in Isaiah 56–66.

[27] Hanson, *The Dawn of Apocalyptic*, the example in Isaiah 58 in which the oracle contains within it the elements of both *judgment* for apostasy (vv. 2-5) and *promise* for those who follow the ways of God (vv. 6-12), 106–7. C. Westermann, *Prophetic Oracles of Salvation in the Old Testament*, 241–45.

by a description of how a man (sic) will be blessed. The chapters following the prologue pick up the issue of righteousness. We find the concept of righteousness is present in Isaiah 57–64, which lends support to the possibility of its being one of the themes in Isaiah 56–66.[28]

Other motifs for consideration as integrating themes include a consistent proclamation of judgment on the apostate and salvation for the faithful. The person who keeps the covenant (Isa 56:6), who trembles and is of contrite heart will have the joy of living in a new Jerusalem. On the other hand, those who follow syncretistic practices and who fail to hear God's call will suffer terrible punishment and have no part in the new Jerusalem.

A holistic reading of Isaiah 56–66 suggests the faithful are also named as the servants. These servants as defined in Isaiah 56:1-8 include foreigners and eunuchs who keep the covenant. Thus, the effect of a community defined by their faithfulness to God meant that Israel, the nation, was no longer automatically the chosen one. This group of faithful are called "servants" and "my chosen." Beuken argues that the identity of the servants begins in Isaiah 56:1-8 and culminates in Isaiah 65–66. According to Beuken, the absence of the term in chapters 57–64 is not a problem being explained by "aposiopesis."[29] We concur with Beuken's proposal.

There are distinctive phrases in Isaiah 56–66 that indicate a single authorship which had the intentional purpose of composing Isaiah 56–66 as an integrated whole. One such distinctive phrase is "my holy mountain" (table V.6). The combination of

---

[28] R. Rendtorff, "The Composition of the Book of Isaiah," believes the theological concept of צדק is to be found in all three parts of the book of Isaiah and acts as one of several unifying themes, 162–64. He agrees with us that the theological implications change in the different contexts. Smith, *Rhetoric and Redaction in Trito-Isaiah*, has proposed unity and coherence between a number of sections in Isaiah 56–66. Isaiah 56:9–57:21 belongs together in one unit, which is supported by a number of antitheses between the faithful and the wicked. Again he examines 58:1–59:20 and proposes that it is related to Isaiah 56:1-8, 68-71, 97-101.

[29] Beuken, "The Main Themes of Trito-Isaiah," "aposiopesis" is a phenomenon in which "the servants" are slowly constituted without mention of their name, 69.

the adjective holy with mountain is quite rare and is therefore significant when we find it throughout Isaiah 56–66. Another important link across the chapters is the play on the themes "I was ready to be sought" and "when I called" (table V.17). The content of the chapters in which these themes are present demonstrates the willingness of YHWH to be there for the people and their refusal to turn to him. Other themes or phrases that may point to an integrated composition of Isaiah 56–66 are "trembles at my word" (table V.25) and "his indignation" (table V.33). We have mentioned previously that the employment of certain words or phrases by themselves does not sustain an argument for a single author of Isaiah 56–66. Any argument must include observations about the complex interaction with these significant phrases if we are to take seriously the single authorship of Isaiah 56–66. This is perceived especially in the exegesis of chapters 63:7–66:24. Particular "words" that reflect a post-exilic date for Isaiah 56–66 are "abomination," "nations/tongues," "abhorrence," "swine's flesh," "trembles at my word," "heaven is my throne."

The discussion above demonstrates how the literary structure appears to be quite complex with numerous connecting links between Isaiah 63:7–64:11, 65 and Isaiah 66. Some of these links extend to other chapters in 56–64. The connections are not simply the particular phrases but also distinctive theological themes that are present within 56–66: the faithful versus the unfaithful; the new identity of "the servant" and "my chosen"; judgment on the unfaithful and a new Jerusalem for the faithful; extreme examples of apostasy; the people's plea followed by God's answer.

The argument that Isaiah 56–66 is a literary unit does not deny the possibility that these chapters are part of a final redaction of the book of Isaiah. We have observed how a number of scholars believe either that the whole of Isaiah 56–66 or that certain chapters of Isaiah 56–66 were part of the final redaction of the book of Isaiah (Carr, Sweeney, Tomasino). Rendtorff believes the whole of Isaiah 56–66 was created as the summation and closure of Isaiah 1–66.[30] Others, like Steck, see Isaiah 56:1-8,

---

[30] Rendtorff, "The Composition of the Book of Isaiah . . .," 146–69.

65–66 as part of this last redaction, together with sections in Isaiah 1. The relationship of Isaiah 56–66 to Isaiah 1–55 is the focus of ongoing research, as shown in the recent articles by Carr and Tomasino.

We return to Rendtorff's proposal. He believes that Isaiah 56–66 never had an independent existence apart from Isaiah 1–55. His argument is based on theological themes and particular words which are present in the three parts of Isaiah. For example, the concept of "comfort," the "glory of Yʜᴡʜ," "behold," and "the accusation of Israel's iniquities." Rendtorff concludes that all the central themes of Isaiah 40–55 are to be found in Isaiah 1–39 and 56–66. He is aware that the word/theological issue can change in each of the parts. For example, judgment is absent in Isaiah 40–55, צדק has a different linguistic usage in Isaiah 1–39 and 40–55.[31] We propose that our thesis fits well with Rendtorff's suggestion. We have demonstrated that Trito-Isaiah was well aware of the writings of Deutero-Isaiah, but he definitely adapted them to his own proclamation.

Through our study we have come to the conclusion that Trito-Isaiah wrote around 400 ʙ.ᴄ.ᴇ. or even later. The main reasons for this conclusion are: first, there is the concern which focuses on foreigners either negatively or positively in Ezekiel, Ezra/Nehemiah, and Isaiah 56–66. Second, the issue of cultic purity, which is addressed in each of the books, but with different recommendations. In Nehemiah, a call is issued to the Israelites to marry only within their own people and dissolve all foreign alliances. In Ezekiel, a call is made to expel all foreigners from the temple service. In Isaiah 56–66, a dreadful judgment is pronounced on the unfaithful, but a promise of life and peace, secure in God's care, is offered to the faithful. Third, is the use of the phrases and theological concepts noted above (65–66). Some of the words are particular to a fifth- fourth-century period, for example, the presence of such verbs and nouns as, "to profane," "to separate," "to minister to him," "abomination,"

---

[31] R. Rendtorff, "Isaiah 56:1 as a Key to the Formation of the Book of Isaiah," 181–89. Other examples are mentioned in "The Composition of the Book of Isaiah," 146–69.

"tongues," "abhorrence," and "trembles at my word." These words appear in the Hebrew Scriptures in the post-exilic period. For these reasons we propose a very late fifth-century or early fourth-century date for the writing of Isaiah 56–66, which is reinforced by Odeberg's comprehensive study. The very strong condemnation of cultic apostasy that figured in the last three chapters of 56–66 indicates a writer who was deeply concerned for the true Yahwistic faith. Because of the connections and theological proclamations in Ezra/Nehemiah and Ezekiel, we propose a similar historical situation.

We have argued for Isaiah 56–66 to be read as a unit created by one person at a certain time in history. A new proposal is that Isaiah 56:1-8 acts as a prologue, foreshadowing the proclamation of Isaiah 56:9–66:24. The identity of the group in the prologue that includes the righteous, the foreigners, and the eunuchs are all part of the same group spoken of in Isaiah 65 and 66. The group is feeling threatened and is facing expulsion and condemnation. We have suggested that this group is confronting the theological proclamations of Ezekiel and Ezra/Nehemiah, especially the messages that want to exclude the foreigner from the Temple and from family relationships.

3

⋯ ⋅ ∘ ∘ ● ● ● ∘ ∘ ⋯ ⋅

A Light to the Nations

We turn to the passages in Isaiah 40–55 that have been spoken about with such fervor as the epitome of outreach to the Gentiles, "The Second Isaiah was without apology; the true missionary spirit was his: he was enthusiastically evangelistic."[1] Smart suggests that the universal note of Isaiah 40–55 that pervades the whole of the writings was reinforced by the phrase "all flesh shall see it together."[2] At the completion of this study, we shall apply the definition of "inclusive voices" from the introduction and assess how the passages in 40–55 accord with this definition.

We note from the beginning that a different Hebrew term is used to describe the foreigners in Isaiah 40–55 from that used in Isaiah 56–66. Isaiah 40–55 uses גוים (nations).[3] From our reading in the Hebrew Scriptures, we know that the nations are treated in different ways rather than under one overall heading: the nations can be judged by YHWH, used by YHWH for different purposes and, it seems, in Isaiah 40–55, may receive the salvation of YHWH.[4]

---

[1] S. Blank, *Prophetic Faith in Israel*, 148. Plus titles such as J. Blenkinsopp "Second Isaiah—Prophet of Universalism" or H. H. Rowley's *Israel's Mission to the World,* imply that only one interpretation is understood.

[2] J. D. Smart, *History and Theology in Second Isaiah*, 48.

[3] We refer later in this chapter to Wilson's suggestion about the difference between the use of foreigner versus that of nations (73).

[4] G. I. Davies, "The Destiny of the Nations in the Book of Isaiah," 105. N. K. Gottwald, *All the Kingdoms of the Earth*, "judgement is the prelude to

Several texts in Isaiah 40–55 are recognized for their message of salvation to the nations. We shall look at each one in turn to explore the pattern of relationship between the nations and the Israelite community.

In Isaiah 42:1-4(6-7) the nations will see the justice and light of the Lord through the servant, but there is no explicit statement to tell us how the nations will respond to this offer. The text tells us how far the salvation will extend, that is, it will extend to the coastlands—the end of the earth, but not what it means for the nations. Even a scholar like Gelston who accepts the view of salvation offered to all, admits that not all the Gentiles will respond necessarily to the salvation offered through the servant.[5] We don't know for certain what the writer intended when he used the phrase to bring forth justice, but it may not include salvation for the nations. Justice may be the knowledge of the Law, which will induce the nations to act justly and release the exiles to return to Jerusalem.

McKenzie suggests that the servant is the mediator of the revelation of YHWH, and this is his mission.[6] In one sense this statement is true as long as we remember the actual task is to establish justice and torah which certainly point to the revelation of YHWH (1c, 3c, and 4b). However, this does not imply that the servant was a missionary in the way we understand the word today.

---

salvation of the righteous among the nations," 330ff. J. Muilenburg, "Isaiah Chapters 40–66," 656. H. M. Orlinsky, "The So-Called 'Servant of the Lord' and 'Suffering Servant' in Second Isaiah," 97–107. H. F. Rooy, "The Nations in Isaiah," 220. N. H. Snaith, "The Servant of the Lord in Deutero-Isaiah," justice in Snaith's opinion means retribution for the nations and not deliverance, 193. N. H. Snaith, "Isaiah 40–66: A Study of the Teaching of Second Isaiah and its Consequences," says, "salvation is for Israel alone," 158–59, 180, and "not all places demonstrate a debasing subservience," 191. C. Westermann, *Isaiah 40–66*, says "through you the nations are to witness light, illumination and salvation," 100, 305. R. N. Whybray, *Isaiah 40–66*, "Yahweh's sovereign rule will mean salvation for Israel and submission for the nations, the prophet's basic message is to bring comfort to the exiles and not the nations," 72.

[5] A. Gelston, "Universalism in Second Isaiah," 377–98.

[6] J. L. McKenzie, *Second Isaiah*, 37.

There is a dispute among scholars about who is the recipient of the servant's task: for example, McKenzie says the servant's task is to the nations and not to Israel. On the other hand, Orlinsky suggests that Isaiah 42:7 is addressed to those in exile and not the nations.[7] There is no doubt in Snaith's mind that the servant's mission is to release the Israelites from exile and bring them back to Jerusalem, which does not include a world-wide mission. This may be disputed, but if one takes the context surrounding the verse, the purpose of the release from darkness is in order for the nations to see YHWH as Lord. Snaith makes an interesting point that Isaiah 40–55 uses עם only in the singular and that it refers to Israel and not peoples in general. This means that in Isaiah 42:6b Israel is given as a covenant to Israel and "a light to the nations." If the "you" in verse 6a refers to the prophet, then it can be appropriate to accept Snaith's suggestion. However, if the "you" in 42:6a refers to Israel, then it hardly makes sense. Snaith has quite a complicated way of dealing with this difficulty.[8]

An examination of Isaiah 40–55 shows at least three texts in which the plural of עם is used: 49:22; 51:4 (the Syriac has a second plural in the first line of 51:4) and 51:5. Having discovered at least three plural forms of עם that clearly refer to peoples other than Israel, we observe that it is often inappropriate to make definitive statements about the use of a particular word across a wide section of a book. In doing this Snaith has to make a complicated explanation when his theory causes a major problem as in Isaiah 42:6a. The writers of the Hebrew Scriptures

[7] McKenzie, *Second Isaiah*, 38. Orlinsky, "The So-Called 'Servant of the Lord,'" 103. Snaith, "Isaiah 40–66," 158.

[8] Snaith, "Isaiah 40–66," accepts the position that Isaiah 42:6a and 49:8 refer to the servant, 157. In a later chapter he maintains that the "servant of the Lord" refers to the 597 B.C.E. exiles that was widened to include all exiles in Babylon, 175. If this is the case, it makes his argument for 42:6 rather difficult if the exiles are to be a covenant to Israel (see argument for the identity of "am"), 175. To account for the difficulty named above, Snaith has the first group of exiles deported: they become the "you" referred to in 42:6a who are to be the covenant to all the other exiles, and therefore the servant is plural and not the prophet, 181.

changed, adapted, and used words as they created new messages for their own situation.

We don't have to solve the issue of whether the servant is speaking to the exiles or the nations in Isaiah 42, but what can be noted is the lack of any overt description of how, if it is the nations, they will be treated within the worshiping community. We don't know what the writer had in mind when he spoke of establishing "justice in the earth; and the coastlands wait for his law." Does justice mean there will be equal status between the nations and the Israelites or does it mean that Israel will treat the nations fairly as subordinates? The context gives us very little more information to make any firm conclusions.

Foreigners are not the subject of Isaiah 44:5, which clearly designates the speakers who claim "to be the Lord's" as descendants of Jacob and Israel (vv. 1-3). This view is disputed by scholars on the ground that it is needless for an Israelite to say the words "I am the Lord's."[9] Nevertheless, we maintain the context refers to the descendants of Jacob and Israel for whom the proclamation is one of encouragement in their banishment to Babylon.

In the case of Isaiah 45:14, the people who come will bring their wealth and be subservient to Israel—a passage with close parallels to the role of the nations in Isaiah 60–62. It may not be a military conquest, but it is portrayed as one in which the nations acknowledge God and are under the Israelite nation. The identity of the survivors of the nations controls the interpretation of Isaiah 45:20. If these survivors are foreigners they will be offered the opportunity to turn and be saved (v. 22). On the other hand, if they are the Israelite survivors of the deportations, one can speak of a message of hope for them if they turn and follow God. Unlike some commentators who see in this passage an offer of salvation for all people, we contend this view cannot be sustained when the context surrounding verse 20 (vv. 18-25) is examined. The Lord is calling on the offspring

---

[9] For Whybray, *Isaiah 40–66,* it can hardly be other than foreigners, 95. Muilenburg, "Isaiah Chapters 40–66," 503–4. J. D. Smart, *History and Theology in Second Isaiah,* 113. Westermann, *Isaiah 40–66,* 137.

of Jacob (v. 19) to turn and be saved (v. 22), and the offspring of Israel will triumph and glory (v. 25). I have to agree with Whybray, the people referred to must be Israelites and not foreigners.[10] The first stanza in verse 22 (Turn to me and be saved, all the ends of the earth) and the last stanza in verse 23 (To me every knee shall bow, every tongue shall swear) appear to be universalistic, but the passage then ends with a direct reference to Israel (v. 25). The interpretation of פליט (survivor) has to take account of its own particular context. Furthermore, the earth might be saved because it acknowledges God as the all powerful one, but this is no guarantee that the nations are in any other than a subordinate role to Israel. On the other hand, Hollenberg believes that all references to survivors in Isaiah 40–55 mean those Israelites who were exiled and became integrated with the people of the nation in which they resided. He calls these people "crypto-Israelites."[11]

According to Wilson, Isaiah 49:1-6 announces the nations as the context for the servant's mission.[12] However, it is not only the nations because the first thing the servant has to do in verse 6 is "to raise up the tribes of Jacob and to restore the preserved of Israel." The servant will not only administer God's salvation to the ends of the earth but also announce again the repatriation of the exiles in verses 8-12. This section highlights that it is through the participation of the nations that God's plan for the salvation of Israel can be achieved. Therefore the primary recipient of God's mercy is Israel, and the focus is always Israel and God's purposes. The question is similar to that we raised above: what does it mean for the servant to be "a light to the nations that my salvation may reach to the end of the earth"? Is the salvation really for the Israelites alone because the nations will see the power of God (v. 7) and release the exiles to return? The implication in verse 7 is that the nations will be subordinate. Furthermore, this action by the servant will cause those in exile to acknowledge the power and faithfulness of YHWH (v. 7).

[10] Whybray, *Isaiah 40–66*, 111–12.

[11] D. A. Hollenberg, "Nationalism and 'The Nations' in Isaiah XL–LV," 29.

[12] A. Wilson, *The Nations in Deutero-Isaiah*, 281.

The salvation offered to the nations in Isaiah 51 (my peoples vv. 4-5) is centered on the law and justice of YHWH, which includes the coastlands (v. 5). This verse does not use the particular Hebrew word גוים, but the text is included frequently in the texts on the inclusive role of nations. There is no specific mention of an equal status for the foreigners in the coastlands, simply that they will benefit from YHWH's rule.[13] In Isaiah 49:6 the offer of salvation to the nations is transmitted through the work of the servant with no further information on the consequences. While Snaith regards the nations as subordinate in Isaiah 40–55, most of the time we are not told any details of their status within the Israelite community. The only clue we have is in 49:7, which speaks of the princes prostrating themselves. No explanation of this behavior is given; it could be showing respect to YHWH or going further to show submission to Israel.

Isaiah 55:5 speaks of other nations coming to Israel because they see the glory of the Lord through the people. However, there is no explanation of the conditions under which they will be accepted after they come. Those scholars who do accept the inclusive interpretation of Isaiah 55 often want to connect it to Isaiah 56–66.[14] Because the message in Isaiah 55 is very similar to other passages in Isaiah 40–55 that envisage the nations responding with eagerness to the display of YHWH's power, we challenge the alleged connection to Isaiah 56:1-8.

In recent years Van Winkle and Wilson have published important works about the relationship between the nations and YHWH in Isaiah 40–55.[15] They recognize the difference in the

---

[13] D. W. Van Winkle, "The Relationship of the Nations to Yahweh and to Israel in Isaiah 40–55," 457. Wilson, *The Nations in Deutero-Isaiah*, 316.

[14] J.D.W. Watts, *Isaiah 1–33*, 245. Muilenburg, "Isaiah Chapters 40–66," 654. Wilson, *The Nations in Deutero-Isaiah*, assumes from past contexts that the nations will be vassals and not equal, 328. W.A.M. Beuken, "Isa 56:9–57:13: An Example of the Isaianic Legacy of Trito-Isaiah," suggests that both Trito-Isaiah and Isaiah 56:1-8 in particular are commentaries on Isaiah 55, 50. M. A. Sweeney, *Isaiah 1–4 and the Post-Exilic Understanding of the Isaianic Tradition*, connects Isaiah 56:1-8 with Isaiah 55, 87.

[15] Van Winkle, "The Relationship of the Nations to Yahweh and to Israel in Isaiah 40–55," 446–59. Wilson, *The Nations in Deutero-Isaiah*, 328.

messages, unlike Snaith who suggests that the nations are able to marvel at the salvation of Israel, but they are not included in it. Indeed, the submissive relationship of the nations to Israel is seen in Isaiah 41:2; 49:14-26; 55:3-5. However, a modified form of acceptance is noted in Isaiah 42:4; 45:22, 23; 51:5 in which salvation is offered to the nations without their incorporation into the life of Israel. Indeed, the nations might only experience the salvation of YHWH in order that they will release the exiles and be subordinate to them. The expectation is that Israel will be exalted by YHWH and will be YHWH's agent, ruling the nations in such a way that righteousness is experienced by them. The nations can be beneficiaries of YHWH's victories over the nations and are expected to worship the one God without the benefits offered to the Israelites.

In summary, any benefits to the nations are subordinate to Israel's redemption. The primary role of the nations is to support the restoration of Israel, to give glory to God, and to stand alongside Israel as worshipers of the one God. Wilson gives a warning about using modern abstractions such as "universalism" and "nationalism," which are external to the biblical material. Therefore, he endeavors to draw his conclusions from an examination of the texts. He sees the nations as governed by God's servant Israel to whom he has given the authority. The universal God has no real concern for the nations except as faithful vassals who know the "mispat" and "torah" as proclaimed by the servant. Zion is first restored followed by the coastlands.[16]

Deutero-Isaiah expands the universal understanding of God both in the use of the creation and monotheistic motifs and the Lordship of God in history, but always Israel is the center as the servant who represents God on earth. The nations are subject to the sovereignty of God: they are to reject idolatry, to serve God's purposes, to restore and glorify his Temple at Zion, and to come under the administration of YHWH's servant. It is important to remember that in Isaiah 40–55 the writer is intent on encouraging the exiles to return to Jerusalem. When he speaks of the nations as recognizing the power of God, it is

---

[16] Wilson, *The Nations in Deutero-Isaiah,* 248–49, 316–17.

for the purpose of demonstrating to the Israelites that Yhwh is the only God and the only one to be followed. Therefore they must leave their comfort and return to rebuild Jerusalem. After wondering if Yhwh was powerless at the time of exile, they are now assured that God is the only God and even the nations can see and acknowledge this fact.

Therefore the status of the nations in Isaiah 40–55 is quite different from that spoken of in Isaiah 56:1-8. One of the differences between 40–55 and 56:1-8 is the use of "גוי" (nation) in the former and "נכר" (foreigner) in the latter. Most scholars assume in their discussions that they are synonymous. Only Wilson notes the difference and offers some explanation. He considers that the delay of the expected pilgrimage of the nations towards Jerusalem after the exile resulted in a changed belief from a corporate hope to a belief in an individual hope. That is, because the nations have not responded as prophesied, the hope now rests on the few foreigners who have come to Zion. However, Wilson fails to explain why the plural of נכר is present in Isaiah 60–62. Moreover, he omits any comment on the גוים in Isaiah 66:17-24 who go out and bring in other nations to Jerusalem. His argument based on the singular נכר cannot be sustained for Isaiah 66. At least Wilson recognizes there are differences and offers an explanation for the employment of נכר rather than גוים, but his argument applies only to Isaiah 56:1-8.[17]

We conclude, from this brief survey and using the definition of "inclusive voices" as defined in the introduction, that Isaiah 40–55 contains a form of "nationalism" rather than "universalism" as frequently suggested.[18] Indeed, the prophet's concern is centered on the restoration and exaltation of Israel, and the nations' response demonstrates the power and glory of Yhwh. None of the passages has a concept of coequality for the nations and the Israelites, and most times the status of the nations is quite vague.

[17] Ibid., 331.

[18] Blank, *Prophetic Faith in Israel,* H. H. Rowley, *The Servant of the Lord,* and *Israel's Mission to the World,* Van Winkle, "The Relationship of the Nations to Yahweh and to Israel in Isaiah 40–55," states Torrey's position "as one where the message of Deutero-Isaiah was inclusive of the whole Gentile world side by side with Israel in the family of the one God," 446.

Those who see an inclusive proclamation in Isaiah 40–55 often extend the same view to Isaiah 56:1-8.[19] However, the statement in 56:1-8 defines the status of the foreigner quite explicitly. The foreigners are not subordinate, nor are they there to stand externally alongside Israel, but they are accepted into the Temple, treated as equals, and they have a choice of accepting the covenant of God. In fact by using נכר, the author of Isaiah 56 has disassociated his message from that of Isaiah 40–55. Therefore, it seems inappropriate to speak of Isaiah 56:1-8 as an extension of the universalism present in Isaiah 40–55, for this deflects from the radical nature of the proclamation in 56:1-8. Not only is the message of 56:1-8 intended to be different from that in 40–55, but it may also be a means of transforming the nationalism of 40–55 into the inclusive nature of 56–66.

נכר is used twice in Isaiah 56:1-8, once in the singular (v. 3) and parallel to the term סרס (eunuch), and once in the plural (v. 6) and parallel to כל (every-one). Verse 3a gives recognition that the foreigner has accepted the covenant conditions as set out in verse 2, but omits any explicit statement to say the foreigner has been circumcised. We could assume this condition, but it seems preferable to deal with the text as we have it.

Arising from the exegesis of this passage, we find the context in which נכר is used in Isaiah 56:1-8 to be unique in the Hebrew Scriptures. In verses 1-8 we have a proclamation in which the foreigner who has joined himself to the Lord is no longer apart from Israel (v. 3). Details of what it means to be a foreigner "who has joined himself to the Lord" are explained in verse 6. They are allowed to minister to the Lord, love his name, and be his servants: all terms normally used of the covenant people of Israel and their relationship to YHWH. Undoubtedly this is one of the most inclusive proclamations in the Hebrew Scriptures with regard to the status of foreigners and their relationship with YHWH and the people of Israel.

One has to wonder why Isaiah 56:1-8 employs נכר and not גוים, which is present in other places in Isaiah. Do we diminish the significance of the proclamation in Isaiah 56:1-8 by our

[19] J. J. Scullion, "Studies in Isaiah cc. 56–66," sees Isaiah 56:1-8 as a later application of the universalism present in Isaiah 40–55.

failure to recognize נכר as a deliberate choice? Unlike Wilson who failed to observe the differences related to נכר in Isaiah 56–66, we are aware that our observations above apply only to 56:1-8. Consideration was given to the question why גוים was used in Isaiah 66:17-24 and not נכר. If Wilson is right and the material comes from the period soon after the return from exile, Isaiah 56:1-8 may depict the singular use of נכר to represent the few foreigners who returned and not the nations as prophesied. When Trito-Isaiah adapted this material, he may have kept the singular to make the message specific, especially if, as we propose, 56:1-8 acts as a prologue for 56–66. The culmination of the proclamation in Isaiah 66:17-24 becomes general and encompasses all nations rather than a foreigner.

נכר refers quite specifically to people who are neither so-journers nor strangers, but to those who come from another nation to live in Israel. In stating that the foreigner is uncircumcised, the writer of Ezekiel is making clear that he is not referring to the type of foreigner who has been circumcised and become part of a family household. In the material that comes from Priestly writing in the Pentateuch, the גר are sojourners who have become part of households and circumcised. In contrast, the emphasis in 1 Kings 8:41-43 and Ezekiel is to the uncircumcised foreigner. By not recognizing the different depth of meaning when Isaiah 56:1-8 uses the specific Hebrew word נכר for "foreigner," we have failed to give full attention to the radical and remarkable proclamation of this passage. The message in Isaiah 56:1-8 opposes the statements in Ezekiel, Ezra/Nehemiah, and yet it must have been important for it to be retained in the book of Isaiah.[20] This occurs despite the knowledge that the Jewish community continues to exclude uncircumcised foreigners. Later writings such as the Qumran and Targum scrolls of Isaiah do not change the wording of 56:1-8.

---

[20] W. Zimmerli, *Ezekiel 2*, states that the only person to offer any hope to the foreigner and contradict the rejection policies of Ezekiel and Ezra was Isaiah 56:3-8, 453–54. Further, Zimmerli believes that the text of Ezekiel comes from a time when the foreigners were already living in the midst of Israel and so speaks to the same situation as Isaiah 56:3, 455.

This is unusual when the scribes often amend certain ideas and make them consistent with their present theology. One must conclude that the inclusive proclamation of 56:1-8 was important enough to be retained in the canon.

Trito-Isaiah had to be an extraordinary genius with exceptional literary skills to confront the proclamation of Ezekiel and Ezra/Nehemiah. It was especially difficult for the radical propositions in Isaiah 56:1-8 to be taken seriously when the Torah was regarded as sacred and not able to be changed (Deut 23:1; Lev 22:10-16). So the use of the root נכר was a deliberate literary device to help people understand the radical nature of the proclamation. Moreover, we note that the root נכר was used in the description of the foreign women (נכריוֹח) from whom the Israelites were commanded to separate in Ezra 10:2, 10, 11. Thus, the writer is emphasising that the wives were from strange lands and not residents of Israel.

At this point we shall look briefly at 1 Kings 8:41-43 and three other texts that speak about nations coming to Jerusalem (Isa 2:1-4; Mic 4:1-5; Zech 8:20-23) to show their similarities to and differences from Isaiah 56:7.

1 Kings 8:41-43 is set within the context of Solomon's prayer at the dedication of the Temple (1 Kgs 8:3-53). Similarities are noted between these verses and Isaiah 56:1-8. In particular נכר (foreigner) is specific to both texts; also, the foreigner has the same opportunity to pray as the servant and Israel in 1 Kings 8:27-30. Israel seeks forgiveness in its prayer, and the foreigners pray in order that all the people of the earth will come to know Yhwh. The new element in 1 Kings 8:41-43 is the knowledge that the foreigner is allowed to pray towards the Temple and can anticipate a response from the God of Israel.

Whether this text belongs to that strand of Jewish religion that welcomed the foreigner in the Dispersion at the time of Paul is open to debate. Verses 41-43 were written five hundred years before the time of Paul, and while they could be the kernel from which the inclusive policy on foreigners later developed, we need to beware of imposing first-century thought onto the text.

In Isaiah 2:1-4 the nations will flow to the mountain of the house of the Lord where they will be taught the ways of God and peace will prevail (v. 4).[21] גוֹי (nation) can refer to both descendants of Abraham and foreign peoples. Here the context indicates the people from a foreign nation, but it does not include specific reference to their participation in the worship life of the temple. Micah 4:1-5 is almost an exact parallel to Isaiah 2:1-4, and the above comments apply to both texts.[22]

The final text Zechariah 8:20-23 has its closest parallel to Isaiah 2:1-4. This passage fits the general tenor of people from other nations coming to Jerusalem and seeking the Lord, but it does not speak of them learning the ways of the Lord and walking in his paths.[23] Nor does it explicitly state that the foreigners will participate in the temple service (Isa 56:6-7), either by ministering to the Lord or by offering sacrifices.

[21] O. Kaiser, *Isaiah 1–12*, 1983, 52. Note 14 on this page contains a summary of the various dates suggested by the scholars for Isaiah 2:2-5. Kaiser suggests the end of the fifth century B.C.E. or the beginning of the fourth century B.C.E., but in the first edition of his book (*Isaiah 1–12*, 1974) places Isa 2:1-4 in the exilic period, 25. R. E. Clements, *Isaiah 1–39*, places Isaiah 2:1-4 in the early post-exilic period, 40. Davies, "The Destiny of the Nations in the Book of Isaiah," also suggests that Psalms 47, 96, 98; Isaiah 11:3-4 and 42:1-4 have a close relationship to Isaiah 2:1-4, 93-120. An examination of Isaiah 11:3-4 does not mention nations, and Isaiah 42:1-4 refers to Israel (the servant) bringing forth justice, which may or may not include equality for the nations. The status of the foreigner is not clear in Psalm 47:8-9, and the remaining two psalms acknowledge YHWH as Lord over all people, whom he will judge with equity. Each of the passages uses the response of the nations to emphasize the power of God rather than to offer equal participation for the nations within the Israelite community.

[22] D. R. Hillers, *Micah*, 51.

[23] D. L. Petersen, *Haggai and Zechariah 1–8*, 316. According to Petersen, the oracle in Zechariah 8:20-23 is part of a larger tradition associated with the pilgrimage of the nations to Jerusalem, which is preserved in post-exilic texts (Isa 2:2-4; 60:1-3; 66:18-24). Our examination of Isaiah 60:1-3 indicates that the nations have a subservient role that is different from the status of the foreigner in Isaiah 2:2-4 and 66:18-21. This point is not considered by Petersen. Also, he omits to include Micah 4:1-5 and Isaiah 56:1-8 in his list despite their similar theological content. J. E. Tollington, *Tradition and Innovation in Haggai and Zechariah 1–8*, suggests that the eschatological hopes presented in Zechariah 1–8 represent the concept of true universalism and exceed the visions of Trito-Isaiah, 243.

A new element presented in Zechariah 8:20-23 is the emphasis on the people coming from important cities: people are willing to uproot themselves to seek the Lord. This action points once more to the power of God as one who can draw people from other nations to his own city (vv. 20-22). We agree with G. I. Davies that this passage has closer parallels with Isaiah 2:1-4 //Micah 4:1-5 than Isaiah 56:7.[24] However, the proclamation in Isaiah 56:1-8 goes beyond these three texts, which speak only of the nations coming to "my holy mountain" and no mention of an inclusive role within the worship life of Israel.

In summary, we find that none of the texts examined were consistent with the definition of "inclusive voices." We agree that the texts in Isaiah 40–55 were more nationalistic in tone with some limited knowledge of God available to the nations. The same point can be made about those nations that come to Jerusalem. At no point are the nations given the same privileges as expressed in Isaiah 56:1-8 for the foreigner. 1 Kings 8:41-43 is the closest understanding in which the same Hebrew root is used and the foreigners must have some sort of relationship with YHWH because their prayers are answered. It is this unusual text that challenges us today to notice the shades of difference in the texts and honor them, without grouping them all under the old heading of universalism.

Two other texts in the book of Isaiah have been posited as universalistic, Isaiah 19:18-25 and 25:6-9. Isaiah 25:6-9 is part of the book referred to as the small "apocalypse" where all people will be welcome to participate in a meal prepared by the Lord—the only reference to the nations is in the parallel phrase in verse 7.[25] There is a sense in these verses that in the eschaton all peoples and nations will be one at the table of the Lord. It may not say anything specific about the present reality, but it is significant in the way it parallels similar future hope in the New Testament.

[24] Davies, "The Destiny of the Nations in the Book of Isaiah," 94.

[25] Blenkinsopp, "Second Isaiah—Prophet of Universalism," says that "we are mistaken if we believe that Isaiah 24–27 is universalistic; any saving action for the nations includes subjection, 49:7; 49:23; 54:3," 89. O. Kaiser, *Isaiah 13–39*, 199.

Isaiah 19:18-25 comes into the category defined by Orlinsky as "internationalistic" because it refers to an altar set up on Egyptian soil rather than to worship in Jerusalem.[26] The Egyptians participate in worship with sacrifices and burnt offerings, which indicates that one nation at least was regarded as equal in role and status before God along with Israel. This is the only text in which the inclusion of foreigners in worship refers to a temple other than Jerusalem. We note that with the description of the Egyptians' participation at the altar set up in Egypt, they are exercising similar functions as the foreigners in the temple service in Ezekiel 44. The message in Isaiah 56:1-8 includes such roles as loving, ministering, keeping the covenant, keeping the Sabbath, and being the servants of the Lord. In Isaiah 19:21 the Egyptians will make vows and perform them. Whether these vows are similar to any of the acts described in Isaiah 56:1-8, we cannot tell. What we can say is that this description of the role of the Egyptians in worship is the closest parallel we have to that described in 56:1-8.

Zechariah 14:16-19 deals with the survivors of all the nations who go to Jerusalem to worship and to keep the feast of booths. The text is similar to Isaiah 56:1-8 in one aspect: that is, the possibility of foreigners worshiping together in the Temple (Zech 14:16). This passage demonstrates a much closer similarity to Isaiah 40–55 than to 56:1-8.

We move to a brief survey of the texts outside the book of Isaiah that use the root נכר and compare them with Isaiah 56:1-8. נכר is used thirty times in the Hebrew Scriptures, of which nine have some inclusive status for the foreigner (eleven places if one includes the parallel 2 Chr 6:32, 33//1 Kgs 8:41, 43). In the other twenty-one places the context is negative about the foreigner and often directly opposed to what is good for Israel. For example, Israel may extort money from a foreigner, but not a brother (Deut 15:3), no foreigner is to be king (Deut 17:15), no animal is to be bought from a foreigner (Lev 22:25), Israel cannot rest in a city of foreigners (Judg 19:12), no foreigner is allowed in the sanctuary (Ezek 44:7, 9), and the ultimate threat

---

[26] H. M. Orlinsky, "Nationalism-Universalism and Internationalism in Ancient Israel," 223.

is implied when Israelite homes and possessions will be given to foreigners (Lam 5:2). The "foreigners" according to such texts are people outside of Israel's life and all contact with them is condemned.

The nine instances in which the foreigner is included in the life of the Israelite community reveal different facets. In Genesis (17:12, 27) and Exodus (12:43), circumcision is the criterion for inclusion in the community of faith for both slaves and children bought from foreigners. Circumcised slaves may partake of the Passover Feast and indeed be regarded as natives of the land (Exod 12:48). Although circumcised foreigners may take part in the Passover meal, no evidence is given to suggest that they worship in the Temple. This particular criterion is not present in any of the other texts (Ruth, Samuel, Kings, Isaiah) that include foreigners as part of the Israelite community.

This brief survey of נכר in passages other than Isaiah demonstrates varied aspects of the rejection of foreigners by the Israelite community or, on the other hand, their participation in the Israelite community. 1 Kings 8:41-43, as noted above, uses the word נכר with corresponding elements of inclusiveness. The assumption that the foreigner's prayer will be answered in 1 Kings 8:43 points to an equal treatment, at least given by God if not by the Israelites. We are cautious about the concept of a linear development or revelation in regards to the equal acceptance of foreigners within the Israelite community, but we have glimpses in Scripture of the changed status of the foreigner in relation to God and to Israel. There appear to have been occasions when some people inspired by God and their situation were able to see beyond their own circumstances and so proclaimed a new understanding that was radical for the orthodox Israelite.

Now we have clarified the nature of the inclusive proclamation and the degree of difference present in the above texts we shall move forward to examine possible other inclusive voices in the books of Ruth and Jonah.

4

．．。。。●●●。。。．．

Ruth and Jonah

We turn to other literature in the Hebrew Scriptures that include stories of foreigners and their relationship with the Israelites. In particular, we shall discuss the books of Ruth and Jonah.

Ruth is the story of a foreigner in which the text refrains from any debate about the inclusion or exclusion of foreigners in the midst of the community, nor is it a rebuttal such as we discussed in Isaiah 56. There are spirited arguments among scholars about the dating of Ruth ranging from a time early in the monarchy to the middle of the fifth century B.C.E., and the arguments for each position are quite persuasive.[1] Larkin is convinced of

---

[1] Discussion about the dating for the book of Ruth has been covered in detail in many commentaries and articles. E. F. Campbell, *Ruth: A New Translation with Introduction, Notes, and Commentary,* places it in the early monarchial period (950–700) with prior oral transmission. He argues very convincingly for an earlier dating, 24. K. A. Robertson Farmer, "The Book of Ruth," 889–946. I. Fischer, "The Book of Ruth: A 'Feminist' Commentary to the Torah?" is convinced that Ruth was written after the exile and indeed may be a polemic against the message of Ezra/Nehemiah and their exclusive policies especially against foreigners, 34. M. Goulder, "Ruth: A Homily on Deuteronomy 22–25?" suggests that Ruth is a late book of the fourth century, 313. M. D. Gow, *The Book of Ruth,* 99. A. S. Herbert, "Ruth." R. L. Hubbard, *The Book of Ruth,* 45. K.J.A. Larkin, *Ruth and Esther,* 11. K. Nielsen, *Ruth,* 28–29. J. M. Sasson, *Ruth: A New Translation with a Philological Commentary and a Formalist-Folklorist Interpretation.*

its post-exilic dating: "In more theological terms, Ruth is said to have a universalism and humaneness about it which set it alongside such works as Ecclesiastes and Jonah theologically, and make it late and compatible with the wisdom tradition."[2] Even if the book of Ruth was not created in post-exilic times to counter Ezra/Nehemiah's policies, surely it must have been circulating and known to the people of the time. Consequently, it can speak to more than one situation, that is, when it was an oral tradition, when it was first written down, and thereafter throughout the following generations. It is on the basis of this premise that we are including it within the post-exilic debate.

The story of Ruth begins in a foreign land, as do the stories of Esther, Daniel 1–6, and the Joseph cycle, but the denouement takes place in Israel. All the stories demonstrate a consequence of this intermingling in society:

> All of them bring together Israelite and foreign cultures, and between them show a range of different attitudes in Israel to foreigners, united by the common insistence that meaningful human relations are possible across national barriers and even that the Lord works to bring them about.[3]

Literature from the exilic period and the post-exilic period can be added to the above group. However, not all the stories would demonstrate the "meaningful human relationships" spoken of in Larkin's quote. For example, the proclamations of Ezra/Nehemiah and Ezekiel do not fall into this category nor does the story of Daniel and his companions.

The interesting difference between Ruth and the other books of Jonah and Esther is that she is a foreigner among the Jews rather than a Jew among the foreigners.[4] Isaiah 56–66 may represent a similar situation to that of Ruth. If, as suggested by Älstrom and Gottwald, the foreigners came into Judah from the surrounding countries after the departure of the exiles,

---

[2] Larkin, *Ruth and Esther,* 23.

[3] Ibid., 11.

[4] Ibid., Ruth "is the only one to deal with a foreigner among Israelites, not *vice versa*," 23.

there may have been more foreigners in Judah than the Israelites who had been left in the land.[5] However, while this can be only conjecture we are confident from a close reading of 56–66 that it represents the views of foreigners who are included within the worshiping community.

Like Gow, I have no wish to postulate earlier and later elements in the book of Ruth, but deal with it as a literary unit.[6] It is possible that when we deal with a piece of literature as a literary unit we are able to make a more informed suggestion for the purpose and dating of the book. As we are restricted by the confines of this book, we shall concentrate our study on those elements within the book of Ruth that speak immediately to the issue of a foreigner in Israelite society. Many other issues and theological points are covered in the abundant and excellent scholarly output on the book of Ruth.

At the point when Ruth arrives in Israel she is known and spoken of as Ruth the Moabitess (1:22; 2:2; 2:6; 2:21; 4:5; 4:10).[7] She has no need to be identified as such before her arrival in Israel, but the insertion of this title now intends us to know that she is definitely a foreigner (נכר). The people, when they heard the statement that Ruth was a "Moabitess," would immediately know from their own history that this was a person usually excluded from their society (Deut 23:3, a Moabite is excluded to the tenth generation and Ruth was of the fourth generation).[8] The Moabites are condemned because of their lack of hospitality to Israelites when they were journeying out of Egypt and because they hired Balaam to curse Israel (23:4-6). By the time of Ezra/Nehemiah the Torah had become fixed and regarded as sacred Scripture (B.C.E. 440). Therefore, the law

---

[5] G. W. Ahlström, *The History of Ancient Palestine from the Palaeolithic Period to Alexander's Conquest*, 822–47. Gottwald, *The Hebrew Bible*, suggests that the Edomites crossed from Transjordan, settling in the north of Judah, with the likelihood that the Ammonites and Moabites reclaimed territories in the Transjordan and maybe west of Jordan. Samaritans also pressed into Judah from the north to occupy deserted estates, 424.

[6] Gow, *The Book of Ruth*, 120.

[7] Ibid., 124.

[8] Goulder, "Ruth: A Homily on Deuteronomy 22–25?" 316.

forbidding the inclusion of a Moabite in worship or community was especially binding. This gave a great advantage to Ezra/Nehemiah who were able to call on the Law to uphold their policy of exclusion.

Moreover, Genesis 19:29-38 provides information about Ruth's Moabite origins. The lineage came from the elder of Lot's sons, Moab, from intercourse with his daughter. An engaging suggestion has been that the relationship between Ruth and Boaz in some way counters the incestuous relationship between Lot and his daughters. Ruth and Boaz behave with propriety.[9] Although the suggestion is a little strange when Ruth practically compromises Boaz into a proposal of marriage (Ruth 3:13-16).

What is interesting about Boaz is that his behavior goes beyond the Law. He is not obligated to marry Ruth by law because he is not a son of Naomi. He goes beyond the Law and behaves with righteousness that does counter the behavior of two of his ancestors—Lot's daughter and Judah who broke the Law. The Law excludes Ruth as a Moabite from participation in the life of Israel, and yet she is counted as righteous because of her faithfulness and her relationship with YHWH. These are important aspects when we consider how it is that foreigners have been accepted into the worshiping life of Israel.

Prior to Ruth's arrival in Israel, we have the start of the family's sojourn when Elimelech journeys into Moab and his two sons marry women from that country. We have no comment within the story about the fact that Elimelech settles in Moab or about the marriage of his sons to Moabite women. What this absence signifies in the story is difficult to conjecture. Did the author approve of Elimelech's move into Moab to feed his family and the later marriage of his sons to Moabite women? In the end did practical necessity override the Torah? Did Ruth expunge Elimelech's actions by her own faithfulness to Naomi? We can only surmise in light of the strong anti-Moabite statements in other literature of the Hebrew Scriptures about the lack of comment in this story. However, this in itself would have confronted the hearers of this story and caused them to wonder why Elimelech's actions were condoned and not condemned.

[9] L. L. Bronner, *A Thematic Approach to Ruth in Rabbinic Literature,* 159.

Ruth would have been scrutinized carefully when she returned initially with Naomi. Foreigners were viewed with suspicion, especially Moabites because of their past history with Israel. A further disadvantage for Ruth was her gender. Women, especially a foreign woman, would have been seen as a temptation to sin.[10]

We note one of the parallels with the Isaiah 56 material, that is, both books contain elements which contradict a Torah law.[11] Ruth is accepted into the community and becomes the ancestor of the great King David. This book, similar to Isaiah 56–66, represents the inclusive voice in the Hebrew Scriptures and stands in opposition to the Law. The use of the term "Moabitess" to describe Ruth once she arrives in Israel leaves us in no doubt about the extraordinary fact that it is a foreigner who is accepted into the community. We are not allowed to forget this fact by its repeated use through the literature.

On the other hand, Goulder has gone much farther than the above proposal and suggests that Ruth is a kind of sermon preached on Deuteronomy 22–25, and in particular, the Torah law in Deuteronomy 23:3-6 is covertly challenged by the presence of Ruth in the Scriptures.[12] Goulder suggests that many of the laws are misunderstood because the person is writing some centuries after Deuteronomy. However, it could be the writer is quite deliberately changing the Law to confront the attitudes of the Israelites to the Moabites and it is a play on the Law. Goulder has pointed out in detail the differences between the law in Deuteronomy 22–25 compared with how it is presented in the book of Ruth. Is it likely that a writer several centuries later

---

[10] Robertson Farmer, "The Book of Ruth," 919.

[11] J. Neusner, *The Mother of the Messiah in Judaism,* Neusner's examination of *Ruth Rabbah* provides the following observation, "Law provides for the conversion of Ammonite and Moabite women, but not Ammonite and Moabite men, so it is in full accord with the Law," 8. This is how it is possible for "the Messiah to come from the excluded people and not from the holy people," 6. Since this law was probably much later than the time of Ezra/Nehemiah, the Torah was the major rule for the Israelites in this period.

[12] Goulder, "Ruth: A Homily on Deuteronomy 22–25?" 307–19.

would not know what the law meant? If Goulder is able to see that it has been changed, surely an Israelite of the time would know. Whether Goulder's proposal is right or wrong, the fact remains that its very presence in the Hebrew Scriptures challenges the Torah.

On the other hand, if the book of Ruth was composed in the time of the monarchy, it would not be possible to omit it later because "the Moabite great-grandmother of David was firmly linked to the tradition."[13] This may be the case; however, the important point is that it can still confront the exclusive proclamations of Ezekiel and Ezra/Nehemiah in 400 B.C.E. We perceive this especially in Nehemiah 13:1-3, which almost quotes the Torah law of Deuteronomy 23:3-6, and as a consequence of reading this law the people separated themselves from those of foreign descent (Neh 13:3). Nehemiah must have known the tradition about Ruth whether in oral or in written form. Yet, he could still deny membership within the Israelite community to those of foreign descent who were committed to YHWH. We return to the issue we raised in the introductory chapter that, while some people want to smooth out the discrepancies raised by this problem about Ruth and the Torah law, there is no definitive answer.

Indeed, while Ruth is excluded by the Torah from participation in the life of Israel, she appeals to the Torah when she makes her claim for gleanings (Deut 24:19).

Another similarity between Ruth and Isaiah 56-66 is the use of the root נכר when the particular designation of foreigner is applied to Ruth in 2:10—להכירני ואנכי נכריה (that you should take notice of me, for I [am] a foreigner). As we discussed in an earlier chapter this particular designation (נכר, foreigner) occurs most frequently in the post-exilic literature. This, of course, is certainly an inadequate reason on its own to designate Ruth as a post-exilic creation. However, it does not appear to have been proposed elsewhere as an argument for a post-exilic dating for Ruth.

In Ruth 2:10 the word play at the end of the verse is fascinating. The first word is a Hiphil infinitive of נכר, and usually has

---

[13] Fischer, "A 'Feminist' Commentary to the Torah," 35.

the meaning "to identify, to recognize someone formerly known, to acknowledge." A literal translation is, "to know I am a foreigner."[14] However, in this particular construction of the infinitive with the ל prefix it can indicate prior knowledge of the person which may be the cause of Ruth's surprise for she had never previously met Boaz.[15] It seems doubtful that the literary construction on נכר (foreigner) could be a sarcastic comment, but rather the recognition of her as a foreigner highlighted the kindness and protective nature of Boaz. He knows that he is offering his protection to a woman from a country that is expressly condemned in the Torah. It appears that this play on the "foreign" status of Ruth is very clever and quite deliberate.

The discussions around the purpose for the book of Ruth fall into three broad categories: (1) As an apologetic against Ezra/Nehemiah around 400 B.C.E. (2) To support the concept of Levirate marriage at a time when it was questioned. (3) To glorify the fidelity of Ruth which either justifies her acceptance into the Israelite community or as the ancestor of David.[16]

A number of scholars support the first proposal as the one which best describes the purpose for the book of Ruth. For example, the theory of the book as a counter to the policies of Ezra/Nehemiah is accepted by LaCocque.[17] However, Rowley

---

[14] Campbell, *Ruth,* thinks the following comes closest to a meaning "no one takes note of me," 98. Nielsen, *Ruth,* translates the phrase as "even though I am a foreigner?" 56. Sasson, *Ruth,* "I am but a foreigner!" 49. Robertson Farmer, "The Book of Ruth," "Why have I found such favor in your eyes that you notice me—a foreigner?" F. W. Bush, *Ruth/Esther,* notes that the infinite with ל can express result or consequence, 123. See BDB, 1, 648.

[15] Hubbard, *Ruth,* 122.

[16] R. M. Hals, *The Theology of the Book of Ruth,* 2. One of the exceptions to any of the above suggested purposes for the book of Ruth is that proposed by Bush, *Ruth/Esther,* in which "the story is about the death and emptiness that have afflicted the life of Naomi," 51. All the other characters are in a minor role and of secondary concern. Yet when Bush states the themes in full he mentions the loyalty of Ruth first, the kindness of Boaz second, the loving concern of Naomi third, and YHWH's gracious provision of a son fourth.

[17] Gow, *The Book of Ruth,* see note 10 re comments on Rowley and LaCocque, 118.

suggests that it could be read as favoring the position of Ezra/Nehemiah in that it shows the picture of a true convert. The problem with this argument is the way that Ezra/Nehemiah insist on the separation of the foreign from the Israelite community. There is no evidence that only unfaithful or pagan foreigners were excluded. No exceptions are given. Herbert believes that the book of Ruth arises out of the post-exilic period soon after the reforms of Ezra/Nehemiah in order to show that believing Gentiles can belong to people of God.[18] The faith must of course be kept free of any pagan contamination, but believing Moabites were acceptable.[19]

Hubbard dates the book of Ruth in the time of Solomon, which allows for the possibility that if it was an oral tradition it could easily have been picked up because it was relevant in the time of Ezra/Nehemiah. If David used foreigners in his army and in other administration type positions, one could conjecture that some of them would become involved in the worship life of Israel. Ittai from Gath was one such person whom we are told was loyal to David (2 Sam 15:18-19; 18:2, 5), but who is named as a foreigner (2 Sam 5:19). There are explicit references to Philistines, Jebusites (the original inhabitants of Jerusalem), and Phoenicians. We have no direct reference to the attitude of the people of Israel at that time to the presence of the foreigners working for David. Hubbard makes a case for the need to justify the inclusion of foreigners who adopt YHWH and outdo the Israelites in חסד (loving kindness).[20] Hubbard agrees that one cannot date the book of Ruth with certainty but thinks that the reign of Solomon is the most likely setting.

[18] A. S. Herbert, "Ruth," 316.

[19] Goulder, "Ruth: A Homily on Deuteronomy 22–25?" "a function of the defensive movement in Israel . . . that Israelites should not have foreign wives," 316. Fischer, "The Book of Ruth," "piece of work against the attempts of the books of Ezra and Nehemiah to reject mixed marriages," 34. Bush, *Ruth/Esther*, believes that based on an analysis of language the book arises from the beginning of the post-exilic period, 30. Bush has an interest in analysis and the purpose for the book is calculated on the prominence of the structural elements that can determine the theme, 48. Naomi is the central character and all the other players are in relationship to her.

[20] Hubbard, *Ruth*, 72–74.

The second proposal professes to uphold the case for Levirate marriage and to show its acceptability by its outcome in the book of Ruth. The situation in relation to Ruth and Boaz certainly makes one think about this law in Deuteronomy 25:5-10, but as Goulder and others have pointed out, the situation in Ruth is different, for example, from that in Genesis 38. The points of contact in Ruth are when Naomi says she is too old to have more sons (1:11-13) and the offer by Boaz to redeem the land and with it, marriage to Ruth (4:1-10).[21] In fact he is not obliged by the law to redeem the land because he is not the full brother to Mahlon nor have he and Ruth dwelled together.[22] A connection may be made to "the regulation of Lev 25:23-34 that aims at preserving the share of land for impoverished landowners."[23] It has been pointed out by Mieke Bal that the law of Levirate marriage and redemption represent posterity and possession of land. Both elements are crucial in the history of Israel and in the social and financial survival of Naomi and Ruth.[24]

The question is raised, if Boaz is not responsible under the law, why set up the story in this way?[25] Boaz emerges as the epitome of kindness and doing what is necessary to preserve the dignity and posterity of Naomi. He isn't compelled by the law but

---

[21] The Law is to ensure the dead son has progeny to bear his name. Here Naomi is concerned for her daughters-in-law and the need to provide for them. It is a shifting of the emphasis but using the Law to draw attention to the plight of Orpah and Ruth.

[22] Fischer, "The Book of Ruth," 38. Boaz is not legally bound to marry Ruth, and neither is the kinsman from whom Boaz redeems the field.

[23] Ibid., 39.

[24] M. Bal, "Heroism and Proper Names, Or the Fruits of Analogy," 59.

[25] Fischer, "The Book of Ruth," suggests that narrations have no intention of being consistent with the Law, instead they adapt the Law to their own specific situations, 40. Bush, *Ruth/Esther,* proposes three major differences between the events in Ruth compared to the events in Genesis 38 and law in Deuteronomy 23. Boaz is not obliged by law to redeem the field and marry Ruth. Second, neither Naomi or Ruth have initiated any legal action that suggests that they are aware there is none. Third, in Ruth there is no social stigma attached to the relative who refused to redeem the field and marry Ruth as suggested in Deuteronomy 25:9-10, 223–24.

follows the right course. Ruth who has called on the law of redemption is providing for both her own and Naomi's future. It will enable both women to be in a secure position in society with status and financial security. We are prompted to remember the story of Judah and Tamar, the ancestors of Boaz. Boaz, unlike Judah who attempted to avoid his duty by the law, initiates and carries through the right action to redeem the land and marry Ruth.

Is it so inconceivable to suggest that Boaz redeems the actions of his ancestor? Another connection that can be made between the stories is the possibility that Tamar was a foreigner, thereby providing a parallel to Ruth whose identity as a foreigner is in no doubt. Tamar is not avowed as a foreigner, but one tends to assume it because Judah was living in the land of Canaan and his first wife had been a Canaanite.[26] Nielsen thinks it is a deliberate stance on behalf of the writer of Ruth, which puts Boaz and his foreign ancestry together with a story about what the foreign ancestry revealed about David.[27] Furthermore, she perceives the story of Tamar as pre-condition for the story of Ruth; indeed it must have been quite familiar as evidenced by the reference in Ruth 4:12. David may have foreign blood through both lines of his great grandparents. A further connection is that Tamar by her actions secured for herself the status and security she had been denied by Judah's actions, as did Ruth who had been deprived by the death of Mahlon and left childless.

This issue of David's lineage is behind the third proposal, which includes within it other related purposes for the book of Ruth. I have put them all under the one heading because they can be interconnected. We begin with the major reason, which is the need to defend the foreign ancestry of David. Furthermore, the book is a political statement on behalf of David's dynasty. One aspect of this in the text of Ruth 4:16-17 is concerned to justify the Davidic male line and glosses over the Moabite ancestry by Judaizing his Moabite great-grandmother.

---

[26] Nielsen, *Ruth*, ". . . it is likely that she too is a Canaanite," 15.
[27] Ibid., 24.

In order to justify Ruth as a foreign great-grandmother, there is a heavy emphasis on Ruth as worthy. She is shown as a true believer, and her inclusion in the community is portrayed as the right thing to do (as opposed to the exclusion policies of Ezra/Nehemiah). Ruth is willing to leave her own kin and cleave to Naomi, so her loyalty and loving kindness are magnified. The language of Ruth "cleaving" to Naomi is reminiscent of that in Genesis 2:24 in which a man "cleaves" to his wife. We are left in no doubt about the profoundness of the action taken by Ruth when she chooses to come to Bethlehem with Naomi and leave her own folk. Furthermore, she receives a blessing as a foreigner from Boaz (3:10), which gives her special status.[28] Gow does not think loving kindness is the central theme of the book although it is present.[29] He thinks that if it was the main theme, then חסד would be used more than the three instances: 1:8; 2:20; and 3:10. It may not be the main theme, but the character of Ruth and the totality of her actions could justify her acceptance into the community.

Ruth's faith in Yhwh is presented in a grand manner. She swears an oath of allegiance to Naomi using the name of Yhwh in a form that is spoken only by leaders of state (1:17).[30] In the one statement she has joined herself not only to Naomi but to her God and to her country. The form in which it is presented fits in with the understanding of later Midrashic material that a person asserts their own conversion rather than acknowledge an overt proselytation process by a third person. This is the case in Isaiah 56:1-8 in which the foreigners, now they are joined to the Lord, assert they cannot be separated from the community.

Alongside the recognition of Ruth as a worthy ancestor of David is the action of God that demonstrates that when a foreign woman was given the role of ancestor to Israel's greatest

[28] M. S. Moore, "Ruth the Moabite and the Blessing of Foreigners," 210–11.

[29] Gow, *The Book of Ruth*, 116. Bronner, "A Thematic Approach to Ruth in Rabbinic Literature," proposes that the theme of kindness is central to the book even if the word itself is mentioned only three times, 146.

[30] I. Rashkow, "Ruth: The Discourse of Power and the Power of Discourse," 32, note 1.

monarch, it was because she had been chosen by God. It is all part of the hidden purposes of God, which become clear to human eyes at a much later time. This is further demonstrated in the way that the marriage is blessed with progeny, which indicates that the divine hand has been present throughout and the marriage meets with YHWH's approval. If this was the case, it would be relevant again in the time of Ezra/Nehemiah as part of a polemic to counter the exclusive policies of these two writers.

The great theological theme of redemption is another suggestion for the purpose of the book.[31] גאל (redeem) is used twenty-three times. If Boaz is from foreign descent (Judah and Tamar), then we have the situation in which a person of foreign descent is the instrument of redemption for a foreign woman and an Israelite woman. For those foreigners who were struggling to maintain their position within the community, this story would help their cause.

In the canonical context in which the book of Ruth is set, the purpose implies that Ruth is associated with the Festival of Weeks. The reason behind the use of the book is that the action takes place in the period between the Passover and the Festival of Weeks. All this supports the place of a foreigner within the worship life of Israel. Not only is the book of Ruth associated with the festivals of the Jewish faith, but through the centuries the book of Ruth has been interpreted with different emphases by the Targums and Midrashic material.

Certainly a number of the suggestions given above for the purpose of the book of Ruth have merit. It could have been awkward for David with a foreign great-great-grandmother, and this story certainly justifies the acceptance of Ruth as a true worshiper of YHWH. During the time of David's succession when the split occurred between Rehoboam and Jeroboam the story would have supported the claim of Rehoboam as the true successor in line of David.

We accept the position that the story could have its genesis at a much earlier time than the final creation of the literature.

---

[31] Robertson Farmer, "The Book of Ruth," 889–946.

Summary

The book is called Ruth when it could be called Naomi, the story of an Israelite woman. Instead it is Ruth, a Moabite, a foreigner whose name stands out in Scripture. We are constantly confronted by it. We cannot escape the fact that she is a foreigner from a despised country. Indeed, her country of origin is named more often than is necessary in the story. Her acclamation of belief in YHWH and her faithfulness and loyalty to Naomi ensure that she stands out as a foreigner who was accepted into the community. Ruth's response in 2:10 is a further point in the story, which by its literary structure and play on נכר raise to the fore that she is a foreigner who is accepted fully into the life of the community. Not only is she accepted into the community, marries an Israelite with community status and of financial worth, but after being childless for ten years produces a son who is the great-grandparent of David.

The story reminds those who want to exclude foreigners of the ancestry of their great king and is certainly picking up a tradition that justifies the acceptance of foreigners into the community. If David's ancestor was a Moabite and faithful, surely it is acceptable in the fourth century B.C.E. to marry a foreigner who is faithful to YHWH.

I am particularly interested in how the people dealt with this story in the time of Ezra/Nehemiah. Whether the book was an oral tradition picked up and written at this point to confront the exclusive policies of Ezra/Nehemiah or written in the time of the monarchy, the fact remains it would have been known to the people of the time. The story itself gives a number of messages to foreigners and Israelites within the community at the time of Ezra/Nehemiah. The kindness of Boaz went beyond the call of duty and reminds others to do the same. He was righteous and went beyond the call of the Torah. His marriage to a foreigner did not corrupt either Boaz or the community, and indeed the marriage of an Israelite to a foreigner was blessed with progeny. That is a clear sign that YHWH approved. Ruth was a loyal friend and committed companion to an Israelite, which enabled them both to find life, security, and status within the community. She becomes a model for others. Furthermore, the book of Ruth supports the cry of the foreigner in Isaiah 56–66 who bases his claim on righteousness because he is excluded by the Torah. These two sections of Hebrew Scriptures are the only places that make explicit the inclusive status of a foreigner within their midst.

Why is it in this story that we have no condemnation of the Moabite connection when this action is condemned within the Torah? Ezra/Nehemiah condemn mixed marriages, and the Moabites are condemned in the oracles against the nations in Jeremiah 48. One has to consider what might be the social situation which prevailed in which a book was originally intended and the later canonical situation when it was accepted into the canon.

We turn now to the book of Jonah because it has on occasions been mentioned in association with the book of Ruth. There are similarities but also distinct differences. A connection is seen in regards to a possible universal message in both books. After our exploration in the book of Jonah, we shall demonstrate the similarities and differences in the proclamation of inclusiveness. The genre may be referred to as story in both cases, yet with quite different elements. Ruth is placed historically and uses very little if any parabolic type features. Jonah, on the other hand, has significant parabolic features with some historical setting. The major difference is that Ruth is a foreigner admitted into Israelite society, while Jonah is an Israelite who has gone into a foreign land. The voice of Jonah will be different from that of Ruth, and we shall try to be true to each message.

We give a brief summary of the book of Jonah in order to set the context for the proposed theme of inclusivity.[32] Jonah is called by God to go to Nineveh but is disobedient to God's call. While on the sea voyage to Tarshish, which is the opposite direction to Nineveh, a great tempest arises. It is understood to be sent by God. After casting lots, Jonah is the one perceived to be the problem and takes responsibility and acknowledges it is probably his fault. The sailors attempt to sail the boat to land, but to no avail, and it is with great reluctance they throw Jonah

---

[32] An excellent narrative reading of the story is found in the following book. D. M. Gunn and D. N. Fewell, *Narrative in the Hebrew Bible*, 129–46.

overboard. Did the statement that the sailors "feared" before the Lord mean that they knew and acknowledged the God of the Israelites or is it still the helpless fear of verse 5? There appears to be a growing bond of trust acknowledged by the sailors and confirmed by their sacrifice of thanksgiving.

After Jonah's rescue by the whale and his prayer to YHWH, he went to Nineveh and preached the word of the Lord to these very wicked people. No call for repentance is offered by Jonah, only judgment. Much to Jonah's consternation and horror, the king, the people, and even the animals repent. In his anger Jonah went out and sulked, only to be reminded by God that it is God who is the Creator and Lord of the Universe.

Unlike Ruth and Isaiah 56–66, Jonah is a Hebrew in a foreign land rather than a foreigner in Israel. God is in control in this book. God calls, sets up the tempest, provides the fish to swallow Jonah. God speaks to the fish who spits out Jonah. God speaks a second time to Jonah. Jonah becomes obedient and goes to Nineveh. God repents of his action. God uses creation to teach Jonah just who is in control of people. Some interesting points are the acknowledgment of the Lord by the sailors and their sacrifice of thanksgiving. The other very unusual point is the role of the animals in the story. Humans and beasts repent, and beasts are spoken of as deserving God's compassion along with the Ninevites.

The historical time frame within the story is set in the reign of Jeroboam II (786–746 B.C.E.) and referred to in 2 Kings 14:25. This reference is enough for some scholars to remain with the date as set in 14:25.[33] On the other hand, a significant number of scholars date this book later because the number of arguments which cover language and possible community concerns all point to a time after the exile.[34] The dates suggested

[33] G. C. Aalders, *The Problem of the Book of Jonah,* 13.

[34] M. Burrows, "The Literary Genre in the Book of Jonah," 81, "the religious situation in the fifth and fourth centuries, however, agrees with the situation reflected in the book of Jonah," 104. T. E. Fretheim, *The Message of Jonah: A Theological Commentary,* 36. J. Limburg, *Jonah,* 31. R. B. Salters, *Jonah & Lamentations,* 26.

have covered any time from 500 to 300 B.C.E.[35] Reasons for this period include such things as a number of linguistic examples that occur mainly in the post-exilic literature. These are listed in the reference below.[36] If it had been written in the time of Jeroboam, there was only a king of Assyria, not of Nineveh, and there was probably never such a role as a king of Nineveh.[37] Sasson reviews the arguments for and against the suggested dates for the book of Jonah and favors slightly a post-exilic date.[38] He dates it between mid-sixth century to mid-fifth century. Further arguments for a post-exilic time are the apparent use of Joel 2 and Jeremiah 18 in the book of Jonah. If we look at the context of each reference, we find the nation addressed in Joel is Israel while in Jonah the connection is to the people of Nineveh. It may show that God treats Jew and Gentile alike.[39] The Jeremiah 18 text discusses the notion that God may repent of his actions, either good or bad. It could very well be that this chapter was in the mind of the writer of Jonah when he created his book.[40] These suggestions and the following ones are pointers to the possibility of a post-exilic date for Jonah. There is the unusual reference to the participation of animals in mourning ceremonies (3:8), which may follow from the priestly theology of the covenant with the animals (Gen 9:8-18). A remoteness from a historical understanding of Nineveh that speaks about the unbelievable size of the city indicates both a distance in time and a lack of knowledge of the area. A suggestion of pos-

---

[35] D. Stuart, *Hosea-Jonah*, "The actual composition of the book is not datable except within the broadest boundaries (ca. 750–250 B.C.) simply because there are no certain indicators in it to date," 432.

[36] Limburg, *Jonah*, 29.

[37] Salters, *Jonah & Lamentations*, 25.

[38] J. M. Sasson, *Jonah: A New Translation with Introduction, Commentary, and Interpretation*, 27.

[39] J. L. McKay, *God's Just Demands in Jonah, Micah, Nahum*, 45. D. M. Marcus, *From Balaam to Jonah: Anti-Prophetic Satire in the Hebrew Bible*, 148. H. Martin, *A Commentary on Jonah*, 23. B. Vawter, *Job and Jonah: Questioning the Hidden God*.

[40] Stuart, *Hosea-Jonah*, "But sharing of concepts is not the same as a dependency of concepts," 433. H. W. Wolff, *Obadiah and Jonah: A Commentary*, 76.

sible Aramaisms in the book suggest a much later date than that of Jeroboam.[41] It is generally agreed by scholars that the book of the twelve prophets, which includes Jonah, must have been firmly in place by the second century B.C.E. because of references to a number of passages from these books in other extant literature.

The arguments on the whole favor a post-exilic dating for the book of Jonah. As in the case of Ruth, we don't want to spend time arguing specifically for a post-exilic date because if the material was written earlier then it was available and known to at least the male members of the community through teaching in the synagogues.

The range of suggested purposes for the book of Jonah is as great as that for Ruth. These will be explored because, as noted above, many voices can be discerned in one story, and there may be more than one purpose for a piece of literature. For some like Knight and Rowley, Jonah was a proclamation of universal intent for all people.[42] This very broad general statement has been questioned in recent years. It can hardly be disputed that God did reverse his decision to destroy Nineveh and therefore demonstrates his compassion for a foreign people, but how much further one can extrapolate to other interpretations is uncertain. For example, Salters proposes that the book of Jonah confronted the narrow nationalism of the Jews and showed that God's mercy and forgiveness were offered to Gentiles, enemies of Israel.[43] This suggestion stays within the boundaries

---

[41] L. C. Allen, *The Books of Joel, Obadiah, Jonah and Micah,* 186–87. A. LaCocque and P.-E. LaCocque, *Jonah: A Psycho-Religious Approach to the Prophet,* argue for a Hellenistic date in the third century B.C.E., which is not very convincing, 44. Fretheim, *The Message of Jonah,* has a setting in the time of Malachi, which he dates 475–450 B.C.E. (Mal 1:2, cf. Isa 40:25-26, Mal 3:15; 2:17; 3:14). His reason for this date is the despair and questions about the ways of a God who appears to allow evildoers to prosper and the Israelites are still suffering, 34–36. Wolff, *Obadiah and Jonah: A Commentary,* 76.

[42] G.A.F. Knight, *Ruth and Jonah,* H. H. Rowley, *The Missionary Message of the Old Testament,* 69.

[43] Salters, *Jonah & Lamentations,* 53.

of the book. Salters suggests that a contrast is clearly drawn between those who hear a response and Jonah, who is both disobedient and challenges the way God should respond. Is it a challenge to Israel in the form of a story? There are many situations in Israel's history in which this message would have been pertinent, but it does not necessarily give any real clue about a specific period.

If, as some scholars suggest, the major focus is not the way that God treats the Ninevites, but rather that Jonah and his behavior is the focus, then we explore messages from a different perspective. Although each perspective may have something to offer in the way we hear the overall message. From a literary perspective the audience is drawn into the message of Jonah by the technique of questions addressed to Jonah. The sailors ask Jonah a number of questions (Jon 1:6, 8, 10, 11), and we as the readers are invited to consider the questions and possible answers. Is it Jonah's fault the storm has come upon the ship? What has Jonah done? Can YHWH do anything about it? In the final chapter God asks a question twice beginning with the particular words, "Do you do well to be angry?" This becomes the major point of the book for Stuart who says that the phrase "what right do you have to be angry?" is the core.[44] Even if this is so, it still encompasses the question that God is free to care for both the plant and the Ninevites. The message confronts the people who question God's ways, and the example uses a foreign nation that repents and receives compassion. The fact that it is both a foreign nation and a very wicked one is a double strike against the attitude of the Israelites.[45] The writer could have used a wicked city within Israel as an example but chose not to, thereby emphasizing the compassion and freedom of God to care for whom he wills. Nineveh or the issue of universalism may not be the major reason for writing, but the fact

---

[44] Stuart, *Hosea-Jonah*, 435.

[45] Wolff, *Obadiah and Jonah*, a seeming contradiction is presented in which YHWH's unconditional threats of judgment are still awaiting their fulfilment and on the other hand the knowledge that YHWH's mercy knows frontiers, 85.

that it is in the story is important. Jonah certainly needs to be read as a unit.

The character of Jonah, like Ruth, is less than perfect but wholly human: a believer and disobedient, angry and obstinate, he flees from the task. He knows the creeds. A person of prayer, he takes responsibility on the ship. He is honest and forthright and remains unrepentant. Jonah acts as a model of someone who is cared for by God even with all his human faults. So the story in itself becomes a message of hope for individuals who have strayed and indeed for the nation. If a foreign nation can repent so quickly and receive the compassion of God, then surely the Israelite nation that is God's chosen one will be able to receive the same care no matter how far they have strayed.

If we look at why Jonah was so upset at God's change of plan, we find a person who was totally convinced that the Ninevites were so wicked they had to be punished.[46] Jonah does not believe that God should deal kindly with the Ninevites when the Israelites have so much pain and hardship. Where does this attitude of God match up to basic justice? So what does it say about the audience from an examination of Jonah's character? Some of the issues might be for Israel a loss of faith in the way God deals with the world. Are the chosen people the only ones to receive God's grace? How can people who have committed sins against other people be saved simply by repenting? Is life worth living when God seems to destroy the only shelter? The questions raised about the character of God and the way God deals with people seem to be part of the book's message.

A number of situations can be identified that would trigger such questions. One situation would be the exilic experience, and another would be the glorification of Israel promised in Isaiah 40–55 that failed to materialize. Both these experiences could raise questions about God in the minds of the people.

Jonah may represent the people of Israel who, in their belief as the chosen ones, have become self-centered instead of God-centered. They have forgotten that God is free to act in ways

---

[46] Fretheim, *The Message of Jonah,* suggests that it is not the foreignness of Nineveh that is the major issue for Jonah, but its wickedness, 33.

that may be inconsistent with human ways, especially if foreigners are in the ascendancy and successful in their world.[47]

One element which is very important is the proclamation and demonstration that God is both redeemer and creator. This theology is certainly consistent with that of Isaiah 40–55 and may indicate a dependence on 40–55 (if not dependence then certainly coming from a similar theological base).[48] In some ways it goes further than the theology of creation in 40–55 in that the animals repent and are treated almost as equals in God's creation.

At one time it was proposed that the message of Jonah like that of Ruth confronted the exclusive messages of Ezra/Nehemiah.[49] The suggestion that Jonah has a universalistic message and is a mandate against Ezra/Nehemiah is denied by a number of scholars: Allen,[50] Clements,[51] Fretheim,[52] and Stuart.[53] There are various reasons for this position, and a common justification is the lack of any overt references to Ezra/Nehemiah or the issue of marriage of Jews to non-Jews. Coupled with this reason is the seemingly different issue for each writer. Ezra/Nehemiah is concerned with non-Jews and their participation within the Israelite community compared with the message of God's compassion on a foreign city in Jonah. Stuart says that because God was sympathetic to the Ninevites this hardly constitutes the idea that all people are God's people. The book never implies that the Ninevites were God's chosen, and Jonah fails to address any of the concerns of Ezra/Nehemiah.[54] So we

[47] J. Magonet, *Form and Meaning: Studies in Literary Techniques in The Book of Jonah*, 94.

[48] Allen, *The Books of Joel, Obadiah, Jonah and Micah*, 188.

[49] Burrows, "The Literary Genre in the Book of Jonah," says, "It was this third group that in all probability was the immediate object of the gentle but sharp satire of the book of Jonah," 105. The third group referred to in this sentence is the group of returned exiles headed up by Ezra/Nehemiah.

[50] Allen, *The Books of Joel, Obadiah, Jonah and Micah*, 188.

[51] R. E. Clements, "The Purpose of the Book of Jonah," 21.

[52] Fretheim, *The Message of Jonah*, 36–37.

[53] Stuart, *Hosea-Jonah*, 435.

[54] Ibid., 435.

return to the purpose for the book if it is unlikely to be a rebuttal of the Ezra/Nehemiah position.

Allen sees the purpose in the final verse (4:11) in which Jonah is confronted to see that God has freedom to offer compassion to whom God chooses and God is not dictated to by anyone, even a person from the chosen nation. Clements and Stuart have variations on this theme. Although Stuart suggests that it could be a sympathetic representation of the foreigners as a deliberate counter to what is happening in the community, he doesn't go as far as thinking it could challenge those of the Ezra/Nehemiah persuasion.[55] I think Clements is right when he says that chapter 1 is important in the sense that it proclaims God as Creator and therefore in control of the world and all those in it. It is part of the total theology of the book, and therefore it is important to read it as a unity. Chapter 4 and its proclamation about the compassion of God for a foreign city is not divorced from the view of God as Creator and Redeemer.

As part of this view of God, Clements emphasizes the possibility of a change of heart by both God and humans. This, for him, is the purpose of the Book of Jonah not a story about Jews and Gentiles.[56] Despite this emphasis by Clements and his avowal that there is no significance in the place of Nineveh, there is an equally strong argument that the use of Nineveh is quite deliberate.[57] Nineveh would have brought thoughts of anger and retribution to the foreground for people when they heard this city mentioned. Therefore, when salvation was extended to a city that had wreaked destruction and pain on Israel, it would have demonstrated the capacity of God to change his attitude both towards foreigners and towards the Israelites. The other issue is the particular Hebrew root used to describe the inhabitants of the city, נכר, the same root used by Ezra/Nehemiah and Ezekiel in their exclusive policies. Clements suggests that if God can offer salvation to foreigners, it reinforces the purpose of the book which is "to show that such a

---

[55] Allen, *The Books of Joel, Obadiah, Jonah and Micah*, 191.
[56] Clements, "The Purpose of the Book of Jonah," 21.
[57] Ibid., 27.

way of salvation was a possibility for Israel."[58] Therefore the use of Nineveh as the town is a deliberate part of the story with great significance in enhancing the theological message. Surely if God can offer forgiveness and compassion to a foreign and wicked city then there is hope for the Israelites.[59] This is reinforced even further with the statement that the beasts are called to repent and may receive compassion from God. The story brings a reminder of the story in Luke in which the younger son returns home because even the swine in his father's house receive food and care. The possibility that the cattle can repent deepens the message to the Israelites that they are able to repent and know God's compassion.

Rather than emphasize the repentance motif of the book, Fretheim believes that the book is raising a number of questions about people's feelings about God, such as the seeming good fortune of evildoers compared to the Israelites who are suffering. How does God deal justly with the world? These sorts of questions have caused some scholars to suggest that there is a similarity to wisdom literature.[60]

Although the explicit issues of Ezra/Nehemiah are not mentioned in Jonah, the message contained within it certainly confronts the actions proclaimed against foreigners in Ezra/Nehemiah. One can hardly have God's compassion and repentance offered in one place and an exclusive policy in another. The employment of Nineveh as the place is important theologically because it demonstrates God's care for a hated enemy of the Israelites. Whether this literature was written as suggested in the time of Jeroboam or was indeed a post-exilic creation is not crucial to us. The book would have been present and known and therefore standing in direct opposition to the exclusive policies of Ezra/Nehemiah. Stories have been used to make theological points throughout the Hebrew Scriptures as

[58] Ibid., 22.

[59] Burrows, "The Literary Genre in the Book of Jonah," says that "people of any land or nation may put Israel to shame by believing and acting in accordance with the will of God," 102.

[60] Allen, *The Books of Joel, Obadiah, Jonah and Micah,* 190. Clements, "The Purpose of the Book of Jonah," 17.

seen, for example, in the Deuteronomic History. So the argument which says that the failure to mention the specific issue of marriage to non-Jews is not an adequate reason to believe that it could be confronting that issue. The story itself gives the message. A major purpose for the book as accepted by most scholars is the proclamation of the lordship of God as creator and redeemer who has the freedom to offer compassion and forgiveness to any one. Humans may not understand the ways of God, and these ways are certainly not necessarily the same as human ways.

The major difference in the stories, as we noted above, is that Jonah is an Israelite sent into a foreign land and not the reverse situation as in the case of Ruth. Further, the role of God in the story of Jonah is far more evident than in Ruth. God is in control and overt in his actions to control the behavior of Jonah. The story clearly demonstrates the universality of God as stated in the first half of Allen's quote on universalism in the introduction to this monograph (xviii). We fail to have in this literature any overt statement about the status of the foreigner within Israelite community.

The common use of the Hebrew root נכר is important. It is one of the linguistic ties between all the literature we are examining. As we have shown previously, the meaning always involves the clear separation of these foreigners from the Israelites. The foreigner is from a nation outside Israel and is not a sojourner as we have known in some parts of the Hebrew Scriptures. Both these books could be used to confront the exclusive policies of Ezekiel and Ezra/Nehemiah, one proclaiming the freedom and universality of YHWH, and the other demonstrating how the ancestor of David, a Moabitess, was accepted into the Israelite community.

5

· · · · · ● ● · · · ·

Exclusive Voices in the
Hebrew Scriptures

We were pointed to the texts in Ezra/Nehemiah when we discussed Isaiah 56:3. The possibility that 56:3 was a deliberate play on the word בדל (to separate) with significant theological implications became ever more evident as we studied this Hebrew root.

We begin by an examination of what the dictionaries tell us about בדל (separate). The general consensus is that the word came into Hebrew at a rather late period and that it was used especially in priestly circles.[1] It appears to have developed into a special term with an almost technical meaning (". . . the technical word for that principle of utter separation which is the core of Judaism and has made the Jews separate and apart throughout all the centuries").[2] attached to it. The verb appears ten times in the niphal (almost exclusively in the Chroniclers

---

[1] W. Baumgartner and L. Koehler, *The Hebrew and Aramaic Lexicon of the Old Testament*, 110. G. J. Botterweck and H. Ringgren, eds. *Theological Dictionary of the Old Testament*, vol. 11, 1–3. D.J.A. Clines, *The Dictionary of Classical Hebrew*, 95–96. F. Brown, S. R. Driver, and C. A. Briggs, *The New Brown-Driver-Briggs-Gesenius Hebrew-English Lexicon of the Old Testament*, 95–96. W. A. VanGemeren, *New International Dictionary of Old Testament Theology and Exegesis*, Vol. 1, 603–5, all indicate and support the suggestion that בדל is a post-exilic term.

[2] N. H. Snaith, "Isaiah 40–66," 224.

History) and thirty-one times in the hiphil (most frequently in the Priestly legal literature). In the P account of creation in Genesis, the verb is used to describe the separation of various elements of the creation and leaves one with the impression that light and darkness, heaven and earth do not belong together (Gen 1:4, 6, 7, 14, 18). This meaning of separation of things that are meant to be apart is carried through in other realms of the life of Israel. For example, in other priestly writings, we find a clear separation of the ordinary people from the priests, between the clean and unclean (Lev 10:10; Ezek 22:26; Num 8:14; 16:9). They are not intended to be together and are meant to be separate. It is this meaning, which is used in the Ezra/Nehemiah texts, in which the people of Israel have to separate themselves from the unclean foreigners (Ezra 9:1; Neh 9:2). One reason expressed for this separation is that the people of Israel are a holy people, a chosen race, and therefore need to keep themselves separate from anything that might contaminate this holiness (1 Kgs 8:53; Lev 20:24, 26).

Isaiah 59:2 has an interesting message that states that the people have separated themselves from God by their iniquities. Therefore the relationship cannot be maintained because of the peoples' sins, which are spelled out graphically in Isaiah 59:3-8. This is a very interesting theological issue when we read of the strong call by Ezra/Nehemiah for the people to separate from the foreigner in order to remain pure and stay in relationship with YHWH. The irony is that according to Isaiah 59 they are already separate from YHWH because of their own sins; therefore, the call by Ezra/Nehemiah is in vain.

We return to explore the use of בדל (separate) in the Ezra/Nehemiah contexts. Besides being used to speak of the separation of the Jews from others,[3] the verb בדל (separate) refers as well to the exclusion of the heathen from cultic worship.[4] Apart

---

[3] Snaith, "Isaiah 40–66," states that "The root, 'badal' . . . belongs mainly to P and the Chronicler." The same word is used in the creation stories to describe the division God creates for the world, "strictly to cause a separation." The root is used nineteen times in the Hebrew Scriptures; seventeen occurrences are in post-exilic texts, 224.

[4] J. Muilenburg, "Isaiah Chapters 40–66," 657.

from one text in Ezra/Nehemiah, they all call for the Israelites to separate themselves from the foreigners (Ezra 9:1; 10:11; Neh 9:2; 10:28; 13:3).[5]

In an exploration of the above texts in Ezra/Nehemiah, we find both similarities and differences in the contexts in which this root has been used. In Ezra the emphasis is on the separation of those who are married to foreigners.[6] This is described as the overt expression of the Israelites' refusal to separate themselves from the peoples of the lands (Ezra 9:1). It is because they have mixed with the Canaanites, the Hittites, the Perizzites, the Jebusites, the Ammonites, the Moabites, the Egyptians, and the Amorites that they have polluted their holiness.

---

[5] P. A. Smith, *Rhetoric and Redaction in Trito-Isaiah,* uses Ezra 6:21 to disprove the concept of foreigners being separated from the Israelites as long as the foreigners were faithful to YHWH. He uses this text to deny the message of separation in other texts in Ezra and Nehemiah stating that "if the foregoing analysis has any validity, then the references to foreign peoples in Ezra 9:1-2; 10:11 have no bearing upon the issue of the background of the statements made in Isa 56:1-8," 56. H.G.M. Williamson, *Ezra and Nehemiah,* OTG, says Ezra 6:21 seems to be a slightly less rigid approach, but in the overall message the Jewish community is urged to observe a strict program of separation in order to maintain its identity, l. We agree with Williamson that it is difficult to deny the message which appears to call for strict separation of the Israelites from foreigners. Ezra 9:1 does not confirm whether the peoples of the lands are followers of YHWH or not. Smith accepts J. Blenkinsopp's, *Ezra-Nehemiah,* explanation of the call for separation in Nehemiah 9:2 as the inability of the foreigner to identify with the collective prayer of sin which follows, 296. This explanation appears a little farfetched. In Nehemiah especially it is hard to see how the message can be interpreted other than as separation from the foreigners, although here Smith believes the evidence is at best ambiguous, 57. In opposition to R. N. Whybray's *Isaiah 40–66* argument, one has to say that in Nehemiah the foreigners are neither identified as pagan or proselyte and, as in other places, he uses an argument from silence, 197, 227–28. Like H. Odeberg, *Trito-Isaiah (Isaiah lvi–lxvi),* we believe the terminology and message point to the time of Ezra and Nehemiah, 41.

[6] Blenkinsopp, *Ezra-Nehemiah,* Nehemiah 9:2 speaks of foreigners in general rather than in Ezra of foreign women, and so anticipates Nehemiah 13:1-3. Ezra speaks about separating from the peoples of the land as well as the specific issue of divorce, 296.

A further pollution is inferred from the use of the word "abominations," which probably refers to the nations' foreign idols and their worship of other gods.[7] This act of marriage is described as unfaithfulness; it is not simply an act of waywardness but breaks the relationship between the people of Israel and YHWH.

After the accusation by the officials is enunciated in Ezra 9, we have an announcement by Ezra in chapter 10 calling for the separation of the people from the peoples of the land and their foreign wives (10:9-15). The success of Ezra's message is the overt naming of the people who put away their wives and their children (10:18-44).

We have no mention of what happened to the wives and children that were put away. One suggestion is that it was a necessary action in order to preserve the identity of Israel.[8] This text along with others (Gen 28:1; Deut 7:3-6; Josh 23:11-13; Judg 3:1; Mal 2:10-16) prescribes against marriage with foreigners. "Their intent was to preserve the faith intact and redefine Israel's identity as a religious community."[9] Throntveit seems to justify the exercise because its purpose is to revitalize the religion of Israel. On the other hand I agree with Hugh Williamson that Ezra 9 is an exegetical reflection on a number of legal texts (Deut 7:1; 23:3; Lev 18).[10] Williamson points out that it is a racial separation, not simply a religious one, and cites the use of the verb התערב (become mixed) in support of his argument.[11] The basis for the injunction could be Deuteronomy 7:3, although the undergirding legal principle is undoubtedly J's prohibition against having covenant relationships with foreigners (Exod 34:12-16). Daniel Smith-Christopher wonders if

---

[7] D. L. Smith-Christopher, "Between Ezra and Isaiah: Exclusion, Transformation, and the Inclusion of the 'Foreigner' in Post-Exilic Biblical Theology," points out that the use of "abominations" is late: 33 percent of all instances in Ezekiel, together within the use of badal (separate) and this concern of separation and identity, is consistent with a group under stress, 125.

[8] Williamson, *Ezra-Nehemiah*, 161–62.

[9] M. A. Throntveit, *Ezra-Nehemiah*, 57.

[10] Williamson, *Ezra-Nehemiah*, 132.

[11] Ibid., 132.

Ezra is interested at all in the question of foreigners, but simply the boundaries between groups within Judaism, those who have been in exile and those who remained.[12] I don't think one can separate the issues in the way Smith-Christopher is suggesting because, whilst foreigners might be of secondary importance, they become the means by which Ezra's aim is achieved.

It has been pointed out that early in Israelite history marriages to foreigners were not always frowned upon; Joseph to a Cushite, Mahlon and Chilion to Moabite wives, Boaz to a Moabite, Judah to a Canaanite (first wife and maybe second).[13] On the other hand, Miriam and Aaron confronted Moses because he had married a Cushite woman (Num 12:1ff.). Williamson says that "marriages with foreigners in itself was not forbidden in the Mosaic law . . ." and later because of danger of leading to apostasy "such marriages were therefore expressly forbidden."[14] These statements appear mutually exclusive and the injunction in Deuteronomy 7:3 is explicit about marriage to a number of named foreign nations.[15] It has been pointed out that the Deuteronomic Law prohibition includes both sexes, which is the case in Nehemiah 13:25, but in Ezra it confines the prohibition to foreign women only.[16]

In Nehemiah 9:2 the statement names "foreigners" as those from whom the Israelites will separate themselves rather than the "peoples of the lands." The latter phrase reoccurs in Nehemiah 10:28 when the story records those who have separated themselves from the "peoples of the lands" and who are willing now to enter into a new covenant (Neh 10:29). It is true that

[12] Smith-Christopher, "Between Ezra and Isaiah: Exclusion, Transformation, and the Inclusion of the 'Foreigner' in Post-Exilic Biblical Theology," 126.

[13] J. M. Myers, *Ezra-Nehemiah*, 76.

[14] Myers, 113–16.

[15] B. Becking, "Continuity and Community in the Book of Ezra," says that the above-mentioned texts only warn and forbid intermarriage, but they do not offer stipulations if an Israelite marries a foreigner. Becking suggests that Ezra is so intent on dissolving the marriage that he is prepared to overlook other features of the Torah, 271.

[16] Blenkinsopp, *Ezra-Nehemiah*, 176–77.

the Nehemiah texts so far do not demand an overt separation of wives from Israelite husbands, but surely the acknowledgment that they have separated from foreigners implies this is the case. Some scholars want to make this distinction between Ezra and Nehemiah.[17]

In Ezra and Nehemiah the concerns about the building of the Temple and the rebuilding of the walls are dealt with first before the books move to the problem of Israelites who have married foreigners. After making pronouncements on this issue, Nehemiah moves to a new concern which centers around those who are able to enter the assembly of the Lord. Based on the law of Deuteronomy 23, which specifically mentions Ammonites and Moabites, the author of Nehemiah broadens this specific allocation to the designation, "all those of mixed race" (Neh 13:3 כל-ערב). The acknowledgment by the people in verse 3 seems to suggest that the people were only hearing this law for the first time. Again, while it doesn't specifically mention divorce, the fact that they separated from all those of foreign descent means that the results in practical terms would be the same. Women and children would be destitute in the society of the time.[18] Williamson says "that there is nothing to suggest that the break-up of mixed marriages was involved on this particular occasion."[19] Rather, Williamson believes that the context refers to their exclusion from the worshiping community. He would be supported in his argument by Myers who says that "only in Deut 23 is the phrase בקהל יהוה "in the assembly of Yahweh" used.[20] Hence the argument is that the legal expulsion of those named pertained to the cultus and not to other relationships because the writer was basically concerned with purity of worship.[21]

[17] Ibid., note 6.

[18] Myers, *Ezra-Nehemiah*, ". . . the actual numbers are quite small considering the census figures in Ezra 2" 87. No matter how small, the consequence for some wives and children is devastating.

[19] Williamson, *Ezra-Nehemiah*, 385. R. W. Klein, "The Books of Ezra and Nehemiah," 819.

[20] Myers, *Ezra-Nehemiah*, 207. Myers appears to have ignored the almost parallel phrase in Nehemiah 13:1, "assembly of God."

[21] Myers, *Ezra-Nehemiah*, 207. D.J.A. Clines, *Ezra, Nehemiah, Esther,* suggests that Nehemiah 10:28 is a sixth group of proselytes or sojourners who

After making this point Myers appears to extend it to the community at large, which is a religious community, and therefore the law of exclusion would probably go beyond the Temple and involve the exclusion of foreigners in all areas of Israel's life.

The use of Deuteronomy 23 could be quite deliberate because of the issue raised in the next verses (Neh 13:4-9): the wrongful treatment of the Levites and the elevation of Tobiah to live in the courts of the Temple when he had no right to be there. This observation is supported by the probability that the Ammonite ancestry of Tobias was well known (Neh 2:10). The use of the term Israel in verse 3 suggests to us that the exclusion refers to all areas of Israel's life and includes the separation of those who are married to foreigners and the exclusion of any foreigner from Israelite worship.

Nehemiah 13 is divided into three parts, which deal with areas of the people's disobedience or wrongdoing. The first we have looked at, which began with the Law cited in order to pronounce judgment on Eliashib because he allowed Tobiah to live within the temple precincts to the exclusion of the Levites who were the rightful occupants of the space. The second wrong is the abuse of the Sabbath, which is supposed to be a day of rest and is now profaned by their commerce carried out both in Jerusalem and in Judah (Neh 13:15-16). Nehemiah shut the gates, which prevented any goods from being transported into the city, and then set the Levites in charge. So the second action of Nehemiah was put in place. The third action returns to the issue of foreign marriage, but with a slightly different twist from that in Ezra. Whereas the concern in Ezra was contamination with the abominations of the foreign nations, in Nehemiah the named issue is that half of their children spoke only a foreign language. Consequently, those children who spoke only a foreign language

---

have taken upon themselves the full obligation of the Law, including circumcision, and had thus joined themselves to Israel (cf. in Ezra 6:21), 75. Nothing to do with mixed marriages, 205. The problem with this comment is the assumption that the foreigners had been circumcised. The above group is not the same as those referred to as the "peoples of the land."

were very likely to be influenced by the gods of that country, hence leading to further contaminations by foreign abominations. Nehemiah's action was abusive to say the least: he beat them and pulled out the hair of some (Neh 13:25). After this abuse the people swore that they would no longer marry their sons and daughters to foreigners. A number of scholars have made the point that, unlike Ezra, Nehemiah did not require them to divorce the foreigners immediately, but make promises for the future.[22] Therefore he was of a kinder nature than Ezra.[23] Another interesting difference is the way Nehemiah uses the story of Solomon to support his actions while Ezra reminds people of the Law to underpin his actions.[24]

Nehemiah finishes with a number of justifications and claims by which YHWH is asked to remember him and one of these is he, Nehemiah, has "cleansed them from everything foreign" (Neh 13:30). The book of Ezra finishes with the bald statement "and they put them [foreign women] away with their children" (Ezra 10:44). The manner in which each of these books concludes demonstrates the strong message and its success in relation to their exclusion policy. The situation at the time appears to have raised a number of fears that called for such drastic actions: the need to keep the religion pure, the need to retain the identity of Judah, and the requirement to worship only the Lord. We know from history that these actions enabled the Jews to survive through many centuries of persecution. The other side of the story in Ezra/Nehemiah is one in which innocent women and children were deprived of security and status, maybe even of their lives. Indeed, most of the condemnation is directed to foreign women and only in Nehemiah 13:25 is the prohibition directed to Israelite women against marriage to foreign men. A famous exemption from this prohibition is the story of Ruth, a foreigner, who was loyal and committed to the God of her new husband. In Ezra/Nehemiah there is a lack of comment about the religious affiliation of the foreigners who

---

[22] Clines, *Ezra, Nehemiah, Esther,* 189.

[23] Myers, *Ezra-Nehemiah,* 217.

[24] H.G.M. Williamson, "The Belief System of the Book of Nehemiah," 279.

have married Israelites. We are expected to assume they are a danger because they will bring the influence of their foreign gods to bear in the situation rather than any possibility these foreigners have become committed Yahwists.

Daniel Smith-Christopher sees two different issues in Ezra/ Nehemiah. In Ezra it is "an intra-Jewish debate while it is only the Nehemiah texts which discuss foreigners in any modern sense of the word."[25] Daniel Smith-Christopher suggests that in Ezra there is a special group which consist of those who had returned from exile. Ezra is interested in defining the boundaries for this group and the boundaries include those people whom the Israelites are not allowed to marry. I agree and disagree with Smith-Christopher: one cannot ignore the end of the book, which has a list of those who had separated from foreign women. This action is both an intra-Jewish issue and a concern for the foreigners who are affected by this edict. Whilst Smith-Christopher wants the edict to apply only to the returned exiles, there is no evidence to support this point. Ezra could have promoted his returned exilic group without calling for the separation of foreigner and Israelite.

In light of the message and demand by Ezra/Nehemiah, it is not surprising that any foreigners who had become part of the faith community may have felt despair. To counter this proclamation of Ezra/Nehemiah the writer of Isaiah 56:1-8 uses the negative in verse 3a (Let not . . .) to deny the demand of Ezra/ Nehemiah. One can hypothesize that the author of Isaiah 56–66 took this phrase (the Lord will surely separate me from his people), deliberately inserted it into the text, and then denied its message totally by including the following verses (4-7).[26] The

---

[25] Smith-Christopher, "Between Ezra and Isaiah: Exclusion, Transformation, and the Inclusion of the 'Foreigner' in Post-Exilic Biblical Theology," 123.

[26] P. C. Beentjes, "Inverted Quotations in the Bible: A Neglected Stylistic Pattern," This particular stylistic device has been called Zeidel's Law after an article written by M. Zeidel, "Parallels between Isaiah and Psalms," *Sinai* 38, 1955–56. Beentjes cites a number of examples in which the actual lines of a quotation have been inverted, calling attention to the content of the quotation and the reader hears something other than the traditional-words, 523. Trito-Isaiah is not using an inverted quotation, but he has the

verb בדל (separate) strengthened with the Infinitive Absolute, "will surely separate me from his people" may be in response to the rigorist measures demanded by Ezra/Nehemiah.[27] Because there is no consensus on the date of these writings, we could be looking at the end of the fifth century (c. 420–400 B.C.E.) or early fourth century (c. 380 B.C.E.). Therefore, it cannot be used as a definitive argument for dating verses 3-8, but it could be one indicator along with others for suggesting a date in the late fifth or early fourth century.

Japhet and Williamson both suggest that the books of Chronicles portray a more inclusive attitude to foreigners than has been previously thought. This view has been queried on the grounds that both the aforementioned scholars have limited the texts which they included in their investigation. However, Dyck believes that the Chronicler has an interest in "all Israel" compared with Ezra/Nehemiah, which separates the "Israelite" community from other people living in the land of Israel.[28] The genealogies used in the different books reflect their interests. In Chronicles the genealogies of the twelve tribes is presented, and in Ezra/Nehemiah the genealogies of those people who were in exile. The consequence for the writer of the Chronicles is a lack of distinction between those who are included or excluded from the community. We have no clear idea why this theology was present in the books of Chronicles. It raises the question of dating. Were they written before or after Ezra/Nehemiah? Was the eventual joining of these books deliberate

---

same purpose when he uses "an oxymoron." In Trito-Isaiah the content of the quotation has "converted" the subject of the verb. In this case the foreigners will no longer be separated from the worshiping community of Israel as declared in Ezra/Nehemiah.

[27] Whybray, *Isaiah 40–66,* is happy to support the idea of this passage opposing rigorist measures of the Jews soon after the return to Zion, but not as late as the time of Ezra and Nehemiah, 197. Blenkinsopp, *Ezra-Nehemiah,* makes the comment that Isaiah 56:1-8 could be either a response to rigorist measures set in motion or a written record of what is already occurring in the community of faith, 96. Snaith, "Isaiah 40–66," makes the claim that Chronicles-Ezra-Nehemiah are "really the story of the rise and triumph of the Jewish principle of Habdalah," 224.

[28] J. E. Dyck, "The Ideology of Identity in Chronicles," 97.

in order to give the different points of view about inclusive versus exclusive policies? Dyck continues with his view that, whilst it appears that Chronicles is more inclusive when the texts and consequences are examined, we find that it is still for the sole purpose of legitimizing Jerusalem as the center of Israel.

Ezekiel 44 has similar theological proclamations to those in Ezra/Nehemiah that exclude the foreigner from the community. In Ezekiel it pertains to the exclusion from the worship sanctuary only. However, it has other parallels in the use of the word נכר (foreigner), the theological concepts of the covenant broken because foreigners have served in the sanctuary and the loss of holiness because the foreigners have been in charge of these holy things. The interesting theological issue is the twice repeated phrase "in admitting foreigners, uncircumcised in heart and flesh, to be in my sanctuary, profaning it" (Ezek 44:7, 9). For the author of the book of Ezekiel, to be circumcised in the heart implies obedience to the Law. However, because uncircumcised foreigners were excluded from worship and therefore unable to hear the edicts of the Law, they would continue to be uncircumcised in heart. Despite the lack of comment by scholars, we propose that the employment of שרת (to serve) has significant theological importance in view of the express command in Ezekiel against the admission of foreigners to the Temple (44:7, 9). Evidently foreigners had been allowed previously to serve in the Temple (Ezek 44:8), but now Ezekiel declares that no foreigner shall be admitted.

In the Ezekiel writings only Levites (44:1) and Zadokites (44:15-31) are able to minister, whereas the foreigner is directed to do so in Isaiah 56:1-8. The knowledge that Ezekiel is reacting against a practice that has occurred already in the worship life of Israel (Ezek 44:8) indicates an acceptance by some people of this custom. It further supports our thesis that Ezekiel and Nehemiah are reacting to this practice with their strong exclusive statements. In response Trito-Isaiah writes a rebuttal.

If we keep in mind the messages from Isaiah 56–66 there could be other issues behind the actions of Ezra/Nehemiah and Ezekiel. It is quite possible that there is a power struggle between groups who have different theological bases. For example, the group or groups behind Ezra/Nehemiah and Ezekiel appear to come from a priestly background who are keen to uphold the purity of the temple worship and set in place the Levites and Zadokites in their stated positions of particular authority and control. On the other hand, we have in 56–66 a group who are claiming rights to be part of the worship life of Israel based on their faithfulness, commitment to the Sabbath, and to keeping the covenant. Before we look at the possible groups that are posited to be in Israel at this time, we need to look at the group called "עם הארץ" (people of the land). Both Ezra and Nehemiah speak about separating from this group as well as using the term foreigners (נכר). As stated in earlier chapters this particular Hebrew word designates the person who is from outside and not a sojourner or alien who has become an Israelite by circumcision.

עם הארץ (people of the land) is used in the singular (Ezra 4:4) and plural in Ezra (3:3; 9:1, 2, 11, 14—בעמי *with the peoples*, 10:2 plural for people and singular for land). Ezra 6:21 uses גוי (nations of the land). In Nehemiah the instances of "people of the land" are a mixture of singular and plural: *peoples of the land* (9:24; 10:30-31, [31-32 in Heb]), *peoples of the lands* (10:28, [29 in Heb]). Other than Ezra 3:3 and 4:4, which indicate a fear of the "people of the land," the remaining references in Ezra imply that Israel will incur contamination of some sort by their association with these "people/s of the land/s." In Nehemiah 9:24 the "peoples of the land" are handed over to Israel, but in Nehemiah 10:28 and 10:30 a similar concern about the need to separate from the "peoples of the land" is expressed as in Ezra. Within the references above one finds three slightly different meanings given to the phrase depending on its context.

One can conjecture about the identity of the עם הארץ (people of the land), and a number of different hypotheses has been proposed. If we take the suggestions chronologically then Ezra 4:4 may refer to those who had been imported by the Assyrians (eighth century B.C.E.) into the Northern Kingdom, had adopted the Yahwistic religion, and who now wanted to help build the new Temple. Williamson thinks there could be some plausibility in the suggestion in 2 Kings 17:24 of a later settlement.[29]

---

[29] Williamson, *Ezra-Nehemiah*, 50.

Were these the people who are referred to as Samaritans in the king of Persia's response to Rehum and Shimshai (Ezra 4:17)? A number of people think it unlikely that the people in what was the Northern Kingdom were known as Samaritans in the period of Ezra and Nehemiah, in which case it is a later interpolation. But for some scholars it enabled the people of the land in Ezra 4:4 to be identified as the Samaritans.

Another possibility is that the surrounding peoples, Moabites, Ammonites, and others had encroached into Judah during the exile and had mixed with those left in the land. Another similar suggestion has been that the opponents in Ezra 4:1-4, who are equated with the people of the land in verse 4, are those whom Esarhaddon resettled in Palestine in 681–669 B.C.E. Clines simply says Ezra 4:4 refers to non-Jews without attempting to say their origin. Grabbe agrees with Clines that the term in Ezra/Nehemiah "is used to label individuals as foreigners and non-Jews with pagan practices."[30] Since four of the groups mentioned in Ezra 9:1 have died out (Canaanites, Hittites, Perizzites, and Jebusites), it could be that Ezra is "demonizing" the others in order to support his actions.

A different suggestion is proposed by Morgenstern who argues for a rebellion of the Jews at the beginning of the reign of Xerxes in 487 B.C.E. that was quelled by turning loose their neighbors—Edomites, Moabites, Ammonites, Philistines, Tyrians, Sidonians, and Persians—against them."[31] Evidence for this is limited, and we shall stay with the general idea of peoples from other nations encroaching onto Judean land when there was an opportunity presented by the exodus of the Jerusalem exiles in 597, 586, and 582 B.C.E.

In other texts in Ezra/Nehemiah the peoples of the land are named as in Ezra 9:1 (Canaanites, Hittites, Perizzites, Ammonites, Moabites, Egyptians, and Amorites) and Nehemiah 13:23 (Ashdod, Ammon, and Moab), and we don't have to conjecture about the identity of the people of the land.

What is very clear in both Ezra and Nehemiah is the "legitimate community is the one made up of those whose ancestors

---

[30] L. L. Grabbe, *Ezra-Nehemiah*, 18.
[31] J. Morgenstern, "Jerusalem–485 B.C.E.," 101–79, 15–47, 1–29.

had been taken from their homeland and exiled in Babylon."[32] This community appears to be under threat from those who remained in the land, and the fear of contamination is expressed in the need to separate from foreigners as asserted in both Ezra/Nehemiah. It is very difficult to discern the exact condition and number of peoples who remained in the land. Grabbe suggests that many of those referred to as "the people of the land" were of Jewish descent from those left in the land.[33] Whether they were seen as contaminated because some had married we shall never know, but certainly they were not acceptable in the eyes of Ezra/Nehemiah. One has to remember also the prophecies in Jeremiah that declared that the ones who would be the true Jerusalem were those who had suffered exile.

In Ezra 6:21 not only those who have returned from exile are acceptable but also "everyone who separated themselves from the polluting of the nations (not lands as found in a number of English Translations) of the land to worship the Yahweh, the God of Israel" (Ezra 6:21). The offer in the phrase applies to those who had separated themselves from unacceptable practices and does not say they had to be Israelites, but that they are a true worshiper. These people were acceptable to partake of the feast of the Passover. We are reminded of Isaiah 56:6-7. A further group is mentioned in Ezra: the adversaries of Judah and Benjamin (Ezra 4:1) whose offer to help rebuild the Temple was refused. In Ezra 4:4 these people are named as the "people of the land" who discourage the people of Judah. While Clines and Williamson say there was another group in Judah who were true worshipers and were circumcised, there is no mention of any people who are circumcised in the text (Ezra 6:21).[34]

---

[32] Grabbe, *Ezra-Nehemiah*, 118.

[33] Ibid., 139.

[34] Williamson, *Ezra, Nehemiah,* interprets this as "those who separated themselves from the uncleanness of the gentiles of the land to seek the Lord," should be regarded as proselytes. He continues, "the Israelites who returned from exile," together with those from any other background without distinction who joined them with whole-hearted allegiance, are the only ones recognized as members of the community, 85.

Just from this brief examination of the phrase "peoples of the land," we find that it can be used to mean different groups of people. Nicholson wrote an article that examines many other contexts and says it was never a technical phrase with only one meaning, but it is quite fluid and changes in whichever context the phrase is being used.[35] This is true for many traditions which are changed deliberately to confront the people with a new and often unacceptable reality.

Within the Ezra/Nehemiah texts we found a number of groups named: adversaries (Ezra 3:3; 4:4), priests and Levites (3:3; 4:4; 6:20; 9:1), returned exiles (4:4; 6:19; 6:21; 9:4; 10:7), Israel (6:21; 10:1; Neh 9:1-2), those who separated themselves from the abominations of the nations (6:21, Neh 9:2; 10:28 includes gamekeepers, singers, temple servants) and people of Judah (4:4). There was both external and internal conflict. In Ezra it appeared more between groups who wanted to participate in the building of the Temple, and in Nehemiah it was more political conflict between the governor Sanballot and Nehemiah on his arrival in Jerusalem.

Conflict is not peculiar to Ezra/Nehemiah, but is found in a number of books in the Hebrew Scriptures. Elijah was in conflict with both the king and priests of his day (1 Kgs 18–19); Jeremiah was in conflict with other prophets and leaders of his time (Jer 37–38); Amos stated clearly he did not want to be seen as one of "the sons of the prophets" (Amos 7). Conflict is not a new element in the Hebrew Scriptures, and so it is hardly surprising to see it emerging again in the second temple period.

A number of studies have appeared in recent years seeking to discern the role and place of structured groups within postexilic Israelite society.[36] We give an overview of these proposals because many of the texts referred to are ones we have studied.

[35] E. W. Nicholson, "The Meaning of the Expression 'am haʾares' in the Old Testament," 59–66.

[36] E. Achtemeier, *The Community and Message of Isaiah 56–66*, 1982. M. Barker, *The Older Testament*, 1987. J. Blenkinsopp, "A Jewish Sect of the Persian Period," 1990, 5–20. E. W. Conrad, *Reading Isaiah*, P. D. Hanson, "Israelite Religion in the Early Postexilic Period," 485–508. K. Koch, "Ezra and the Origins of Judaism," 173–97. A. Rofé, "Isaiah 66:1-4," 205–17. J. Weinberg, *The Citizen-Temple Community*.

Isaiah 56–66 has been posited as the genesis for two particular groups: the Pharisees (Blenkinsopp, Rofé) and the Samaritans (Talmon, Barker) both of whom become a major power in later Israelite society. On the other hand, the radical nature of the community in Isaiah 56:1-8 may have been such that it was doomed to extinction or had to compromise to survive in some less inclusive form. In the final analysis, because of the general lack of historical information for fifth to third centuries B.C.E., we will probably only be able to make tentative suggestions.

Hanson first raised the issue when he designated two major parties, Levites (visionaries) and Zadokites (realists), who were in conflict in the early post-exilic period. It was the Levitical or Visionary party that he argued played a significant role in the development of apocalyptic eschatology.[37] He makes the point that the names given to the parties really only refer to "tendencies." While the description may only be a "tendency," the concept of parties used throughout his work suggests two very precise entities.

The identities of these parties are contained within the post-exilic books, Isaiah 56–66, Ezekiel 40–48, Haggai, Nehemiah, and Zechariah. An examination of the oracles in Isaiah 56–66 by Hanson apparently demonstrates the concerns of a "visionary" (Levitical–prophetic) group who oppose the "hierocratic" (priestly) group's cultic orthodoxy. Hanson gives a brief overview of the differences between these two groups of people with the prophetic material of Isaiah and Zechariah examined in far greater detail than the other books.[38] Whether the Levites could have instituted such an inclusive proclamation as that which appears in Isaiah 56–66 is debatable. As an order of priests, they would have had to move a long way theologically to accept eunuchs and foreigners into the worshiping community. Indeed, while the status of the Levites within the Israelite community over the centuries is disputed, there is agreement

---

[37] P. D. Hanson, *The Dawn of Apocalyptic,* says, "For 'visionary' and 'realistic' do not designate rigid parties, but rather theological tendencies which can be traced through the literature of the post-exilic period," 72, note 44.

[38] Hanson, *The Dawn of Apocalyptic,* 43ff.

that they did have priestly functions.[39] On the other hand, if they were marginalized, they may have been able to encompass other people who were suffering the same treatment. We have no direct evidence that the Levites were the writers behind the proclamation in Isaiah 56–66. However, we agree with Hanson that to read Ezekiel and Nehemiah alongside of 56–66 clearly suggests two opposing viewpoints.

Did the development of two groups within Judaism, the Pharisees and Sadducees, which had become defined by the time of the Roman era, have its roots in the Babylonian exile? It is suggested that Trito-Isaiah plays an important part in tracing this development. Isaiah 56:1-8, 65, 66 give evidence of conflict between groups which increased in post-exilic society—a society no longer held together by a king. Isaiah 66:1-5 presupposes, "the existence of a pietistic and prophetic-eschatological group whose relations with the parent body have been at least temporarily severed."[40]

According to Blenkinsopp this group ultimately appeared as the Pharisees. The study for this analysis of the post-exilic situation is based on the sociological theories of Weber and Troelscht. However, Blenkinsopp agrees that there are often reservations when sociological theories are applied to material which has within it many uncertainties about the historical situation. In the final resort he claims that the climate was conducive to the emergence of sectarianism and ultimately to the formation of the Pharisees and Sadducees as distinct groups.

Rofé has a similar position to that of Blenkinsopp, but he does acknowledge a third group who formed an institution of proselytism (Isa 56:1-8).[41] Like Blenkinsopp, he argues that the aristocracy of Jerusalem became the Sadducees, while the group who are depicted in Nehemiah 9:2; 10:28; 13:3; Ezra 6:21; 9:1; 10:8, 11 became the Pharisees. Isaiah 66:3 is a crucial text in

---

[39] *Anchor Bible Dictionary*, 297–310. The reconstruction of the history of the Levitical movement is fraught with difficulty. What is not in dispute is their function as priests although it could be a lowly role. R. De Vaux, *Ancient Israel: Its Life and Institutions*, 358–71.

[40] Blenkinsopp, "A Jewish Sect of the Persian Period," 11.

[41] J. Rofé, "Isaiah 66:1-4," 217.

discerning the start of the division between the Pharisees and Sadducees. We see here marked opposition to the priestly supremacy in Jerusalem, and a clear picture of conflict arises when this passage is linked with others in Malachi, Nehemiah, and Ezra. This group (pre-Pharisaic) is opposed to the practices of the priestly party in Jerusalem accusing them of apostasy and idolatry (65:3-5, 11; 66:3). However, the group is not opposed to the cult, only to wrong practice.

The foreigner is allowed to join the Israelite by faith and not by marriage. This denomination clearly delineates itself from its environment by prohibiting mixed marriages on the one hand, and by the formation of an institutionalized body of נלוים —"Gentiles who join themselves to the Lord"—on the other.[42]

Rofé accounts for the different views on marriage and foreigners in the Ezra/Nehemiah texts by suggesting that Trito-Isaiah kept silence on the issue of mixed marriages because his view did not coincide with that of Ezra and Nehemiah.

The suggestions offered above by Rofé and Blenkinsopp need further work to establish their certainty. We refer to the exegetical work we have done in Isaiah 56–66 in which the possibility of a group/denomination which is both against mixed marriages and yet allows foreigners to belong to the faith community was not apparent. Neither Blenkinsopp nor Rofé make any reference to Ezekiel 44 with its clear mandate to expel foreigners from the temple service.

The Samaritans are another group whose roots are traced back to the second temple period. Talmon proposes a structure which consists of three main groups designated the credal national (inner group), national (in-group), credal-ethnic-foreign (out-group).[43] The "inner group" were those who had experienced exile and the need to maintain a clear identity by strict adherence to the Law. It was this need that set them apart from those who had remained in the land. The conflict arose when the returned exiles refused the offer of those who had remained in the land (in-group) to help in the rebuilding of the Temple. Again they

---

[42] Ibid., 217.

[43] S. Talmon, "The Emergence of Jewish Sectarianism in the Early Second Temple Period," 599.

were refused participation in the building program in the time of Nehemiah and the split became permanent (a position almost parallel to that of Snaith discussed below). This is recorded in Malachi 3:13-21. These rejected ones are those who abided in the word of God (Isa 66:5; 65:11). Later they became the Samaritans who struck out on their own and built a rival temple on Mount Gerizim. The credal-ethnic-foreign group is not discussed in Talmon's work, but we assume it is the group referred to in Isaiah 56:1-8. So the difference between Blenkinsopp/Rofé and Talmon is that the former see the division and growth of the Pharisees and Sadducees in the early post-exilic period while Talmon suggests the division was in the late fifth century B.C.E. and led to the final breach between the Samaritans and Jews. Further, Talmon and Rofé account for the inclusive nature of one group by designating them the "credal-ethnic-foreign" group or the "institution of proselytism." It seems strange that they make no further reference to this inclusive group or suggest where it might fit into future Jewish society.

Snaith has a similar picture of the period in which the people left in the land come into conflict with the returned exiles. He suggests that during the time of Haggai there were differences initially which later were settled amicably. When Nehemiah came on his first visit to Jerusalem (445 B.C.E.), he accepted the mixed marriages, but on his return in 426 B.C.E. a different political situation prevailed, and he enforced the "separation" policy, which was further reinforced by Ezra in 397 B.C.E. (Snaith's dating).[44]

In opposition to Talmon's analysis, Koch proposes that Ezra spoke only against mixed marriages with Canaanites, Hittites, Perizzites, and Jebusites, but not the Samaritans. The Samaritans

---

[44] Snaith, "Isaiah 40–66," 244–62. Smith, *Rhetoric and Redaction in Trito-Isaiah,* has argued that the separation policy that we perceive in Ezra/Nehemiah is not really present in these books. He uses Ezra 6:21 to interpret the remaining texts in which the foreigners, if faithful, are acceptable, 56–59. Williamson, *Ezra, Nehemiah,* disagrees with Smith's interpretation of these passages and is convinced that the fear of assimilation into the surrounding cultures is the reason behind the separation policy of foreigners from Jews, 160.

were still regarded by Ezra as the people from the Northern Kingdom and therefore acceptable into the community. Ezra's purpose on his return to Jerusalem was to build up the twelve tribes of Israel including the later Samaritans. Mount Zion was the focus for the new Israel and the Law enabled the people to live in holiness.

Koch's study focuses on the origins of Judaism and whether they began in the time of Ezra. By his own definition of the terms "Israelite" and "Jew," Ezra is defined as an Israelite.[45] Therefore the move from ancient Israel to Judaism took place later than the time of Ezra. However, he still wants to claim that Ezra's emphasis on the Law became not only a major component for later Judaism but for other movements as well.[46] He is not interested in the discussion of different groups that appear to be present in the second temple period nor their possible origin in the priestly party. His study demonstrates the difficulty in the search for specific origins for the different movements that appear later in the life of Israel.

Further proposals have arisen about the nature and roles of certain groups in fifth-century Israel based on concepts current in other Middle East countries of the time. A study (Eskenazi) of the role of the Temple in Achaemenid Mesopotamia has demonstrated a form of socio-political structure grouped around particular ancestral houses. Responsibility for the organization of the Temple and economic activities was in the hands of an assembly presided over by a dean. Accordingly, this concept was adapted by returned exiles after they acquired land and control of the Temple.[47]

---

[45] For Koch, "Ezra and the Origins of Judaism," the Israelites are an ethnic and political unity, bound by geographical facts, united by a joint cultus, and focused on the Temple. On the other hand, Jews are members of a community dispersed in the *galuth* without joint political or cultic activities, united in obedience towards the Torah and focused on the synagogue, 197.

[46] Ibid. "If he was using the Torah as a book of promise then he (Ezra) was the predecessor of apocalyptic too," 197.

[47] T. C. Eskenazi, "Current Perspectives on Ezra-Nehemiah and the Persian Period," 59–86.

Weinberg speaks of a civic-temple community established in Jerusalem. Based on evidence from the Ezra texts, he proposes a group which had returned from Babylon and became a semi-autonomous temple-community that had considerable control and power.[48] First, this group had to secure the land that had been lost when the Israelites had been taken to Babylon, and secondly, they had to rebuild the Temple. Consequently, conflict arose in Jerusalem as depicted in the Ezra/Nehemiah texts because the Judaean structure included people who distanced themselves from all who did not belong to the civic-temple community. How this occurs for Weinberg is unclear. Earlier we noted that Snaith suggested this group of returned exiles had the status and support of the Persians, which thus enabled them to take control. Weinberg gives no comparable evidence to support his claim for either the takeover of the land or the Temple.

Earlier Blenkinsopp wrote about the roots of Pharisees and Sadducees and in a later article proposed a view similar to that of Weinberg where a group developed

> their own assembly organized according to ancestral houses including free, property-owning citizens and temple personnel, under the leadership of tribal elders and the supervision of an imperial representative, in a cohesive social entity which, while allowing for additional adherents, was jealously protective of its status and privileges.[49]

Blenkinsopp observes the reference to חרדים (trembling ones) in Isaiah and Ezra. He also notes that the term appears to describe two different groups; the ostracized prophetic-eschatological group of Isaiah 56–66 and the group in Ezra who imposed a rigorist interpretation of the Law.[50] However, we are warned by Blenkinsopp not to set these groups against each other. His arguments against the division of the two descriptions above are these: both groups were present in the Qumran

---

[48] Weinberg, *The Citizen-Temple Community*, 67.
[49] J. Blenkinsopp, "Temple and Society in Achaemenid Judah," 53.
[50] Blenkinsopp, "A Jewish Sect of the Persian Period," 17.

community; there is no evidence to show that Ezra was anti-prophetic or anti-eschatological; opponents were in the ranks of the priesthood and related specifically to the addiction to syncretistic cults. We disagree with Blenkinsopp and accept the evidence of the texts in Ezra that depict a group rigid in its adherence to the Law. This group is inconsistent with the description of the group in Isaiah 56, 65, and 66.

Blenkinsopp is critical of Weinberg's theory because the texts do not provide us with the information we need to make a comparison. On the other hand, Blenkinsopp proposes there was a social and economic elite group in the province (Neh 5:1, 17) which constituted its own assembly and was jealously protective of its status and privileges. The differences between Weinberg and Blenkinsopp appear minor, and the arguments against Weinberg seem to hold equally against Blenkinsopp. That is, there is a lack of evidence in Judaean literature to support such a concept and no necessity to interpret the function and significance of the Jerusalem Temple in light of the Persian Empire. Other arguments against a civic-temple community that is supposedly in control of the Temple are again based on lack of evidence. For example, one such argument suggests that participation in the temple community was dependent on owning property,[51] but how had the returned exiles gained control of the land? This proposal while it answers some questions appears to raise a lot more uncertainties, and there is a lack of evidence for many of its suggestions.

Arising from the method known as "reader-response," Conrad developed the argument for a minority group who were confronting another group within the community.[52] The enmity between the factions is so great that it has resulted in murder. By the use of the first-person plural, the implied audience speaks in Isaiah 1, 59, 63, and 64. The "we" becomes the group which is speaking out for its survival against those who are depicted as unfaithful to Yhwh. This literary device certainly appears to support Conrad's proposal. However, while Conrad

---

[51] R. P. Bedford, "On Models and Texts: A Response to Blenkinsopp and Petersen," 155–62.

[52] Conrad, *Reading Isaiah*, 95.

supports the possibility of conflicting groups, he is not interested in the identity of either of these groups.

In summary, we agree that there were groups of people who held differing theological positions. However, whether these groups functioned as fully organized systems such as we understand by the term "parties" is not clear from the texts. The examination of these studies has demonstrated the difficulty of proving the identity of a particular group from the few texts we have available to us. Indeed, the same texts, Trito-Isaiah, Malachi, Ezra, and Nehemiah have been used to argue the case for the genesis of Pharisees, Samaritans, Judaism, or a civic-temple community. This in itself points to the lack of evidence that could confirm one specific group.

Not everyone agrees that Trito-Isaiah, Malachi, Nehemiah, and Ezra show opposition to priestly supremacy. Indeed some scholars make a case in which Ezra and Nehemiah are in agreement with the priestly view. We consider the proclamations in Isaiah 56–66 and Malachi to be in opposition to the priestly group.

The evidence for or against the roots of sectarianism beginning in the second temple period is sparse in the post-exilic texts. As Blenkinsopp suggests, it may be "that the climate was conducive to the emergence of sectarianism and ultimately the forming of the Pharisees and Sadducees."[53] A similar argument holds for the suggestion of a Samaritan/Jewish schism having its roots in this period. The lack of evidence for a civic-temple community is even more apparent than for the above suggestions.

Therefore, dogmatic statements on the genesis of a particular group in the fifth century are inappropriate. However, it may be acceptable to recognize the possibility that any one of the groups mentioned in these studies could have their genesis in fifth-century Israel. The important issue for us is to note how the inclusive proclamation of Isaiah 56–66 has failed to survive into any later formal group within Jewish society. Although both Rofé and Talmon make mention of a third group that appears to be those referred to in Isaiah 56:1-8, neither of these

---

[53] Blenkinsopp, "A Jewish Sect of the Persian Period," 19.

scholars pursues the issue to any conclusion. They both believe the identity of this third group is referred to only in 56:1-8. No consideration is given to the possibility of an intentional construction of Isaiah 56–66, which reveals the requirements for a new community of YHWH's people.

The phrase "עם הארץ" (people of the land) appeared fluid in its meaning and use by these writers, and one could not give a definitive interpretation about the identity of the group. The best way is to use the context and endeavor not to impose one's own agenda on the text. We know from the literature that the priestly group appeared to be dominant through the fourth to third century B.C.E. The Hasidim (Pharisees) are named from the second century onwards as playing an important role in the life of Israel. Nevertheless, we are left in no doubt after examining the texts of Ezra/Nehemiah and Ezekiel that there was a clear policy of exclusion given by these writers. The emphasis and context might change slightly in each of the books, but the use of the Hebrew root בדל (separate) leaves us in no doubt about the intention to separate those of foreign descent from the Israelites.

6

....●●●●....

Conclusion and Implications
for Today

A wide diversity of voices is heard in the Hebrew Scriptures. The voices of those who are included (Ruth), those who want to be included in the Israelite community (foreigners and eunuchs), and the voices of those who want to exclude foreigners from the Israelite community (Ezra, Nehemiah, Ezekiel 44). This study has shown texts that offer and speak of inclusion for the foreigner within the Israelite community in a manner which is quite radical. On the other hand, there are voices that speak of total exclusion of the foreigner and that appear cruel in their announcements of separation for those Israelites who are already married to foreigners and who have children. In between there are many voices that offer the knowledge of YHWH to the nations in which their relationship is not clearly defined. In other texts the offer of justice includes a subordinate role for the nations in which they will bring their wealth and bow down before the Israelites. There is the unusual voice in 1 Kings 8:41-44 that gives foreigners the right to pray to YHWH, and this right includes the expectation that their prayer will be answered. Isaiah 19 gives an overt message that confirms that foreigners are able to worship Yahweh, the God of Israel, on alien soil.

The view of God as the universal one is undoubtedly verified in the Hebrew Scriptures. Genesis 1–3 declares that YHWH is Creator of the world, and this is reiterated time and again in Isaiah 40–55. God is not only creator of the world but also Lord of History, inasmuch as the way God can use the nations, including Israel, for his own purposes. The nations were used to bring both judgment on Judah when they were taken into exile by Nebuchadnezzar and salvation when Cyrus was used to bring release for the exiles. God is portrayed as one who can have compassion on foreigners and will bring them to "my holy mountain" (Isa 56:1-8). Within this role God has control and care of both creation and peoples.

God is a universal God. This is not in dispute, but when people respond they form groups which have different criteria for inclusion. This leads to particularism within human communities.[1] Ruether puts this concept slightly differently when she talks about seeing "ourselves as children of the one God from whom all peoples spring." In response, "people have shaped themselves into distinctive historical communities."[2] This issue of groups or communities setting limits to membership has both positive and negative consequences. For the Jews their clearly marked boundaries, such as circumcision and obedience to the Torah, were crucial to their survival as a race as they were scattered across the world.[3] The negative side to particularism is when a specific group wants power or dominance in a situation resulting in war or persecution. We see this all too clearly in our present world situation in which nationalism has become a driving force for evil (Balkans, Ireland, Rwanda).

A further point to be made about setting boundaries is that every religious group is exclusive in one way or another. Christians have appeared to be on the high moral ground at times when they make claims for universalism. They may be universal in their desire to reach out to all people, but exclusive at the point where each denomination has criteria for membership of their particular gathering. For example, in today's world many churches have certain statements or, in the case of the Uniting Church in Australia, a Basis of Union which set out the criteria

---

[1] J. D. Levenson, "The Universal Horizon of Biblical Particularism," 169.

[2] R. R. Ruether and H. J. Ruether, *The Wrath of Jonah*, 245.

[3] Both Levenson, "The Universal Horizon of Biblical Particularism," 168, and Ruether, *The Wrath of Jonah*, 245, raise questions about the modern ethic that advocates a thorough-going egalitarianism which would undermine Jewish existence.

for belonging to the church. Basic to most churches is the person's avowal of faith in Christ, the authority of Scripture, and the creeds. Very few, if any, churches set down in these documents criteria about the sort of person who can belong within the community, for example, single parent, divorcee, or homosexual. These sorts of distinctions are named as a result, in most cases, of reading the Bible and making consequent claims for their exclusion from the community. It is interesting that the Uniting Church, for example, holding to the Basis of Union, accepts all people as full members. The Basis says nothing about the sexual orientation of the person or his/her status as a single parent or past criminal, only that a person who truly turns and follows Christ is accepted as a member. This is the same ground on which the foreigner fought for the right to remain within the post-exilic community.

Genesis 1–11 speaks of the creation of the world and people in an universal sense before the Scriptures speak about Israel as the chosen race (Genesis 12).[4] In this chapter God makes promises to Abraham about Israel's future as a powerful nation, and in response Abraham moves out in faith. Prior to the covenant with Abraham, we note, for example, that the Noah covenant was universal (Genesis 8–9). Furthermore, even after Israel was chosen, the Scriptures record a number of non-Israelites who revered YHWH and who were honored in the tradition: Jethro (Exod 18), Balaam (Num 22–24), Rahab (Josh 2), Naaman (2 Kgs 5), Job, Cyrus (Isa 44:24–45:10).[5] A significant block of the Hebrew Scriptures (Proverbs, Job, and Ecclesiastes) never refers to the people of Israel, Exodus, the covenant of Sinai, or the gift of the land.[6] This appears to indicate that not all writers of the Hebrew Scriptures held these traditions as essential when writing their own works.

However, there is the proclamation in the Hebrew Scriptures that the Jews are the chosen race and various rational explanations have been given to explain this claim. Levenson[7] and Ruether offer similar explanations. The people of Israel were

[4] Levenson, "The Universal Horizon of Biblical Particularism," 147.
[5] Ibid., 148.
[6] Ibid., 149.
[7] Ibid., 155.

chosen for a purpose, to be the witnesses and beneficiaries of universalism. Ruether suggests that "the universalistic tradition affirms Jewish particularity in solidarity with the particularity to other people. Concern for the Jewish distinctiveness means granting an equal concern for the rights of other people to exist in distinct ways."[8]

Both these explanations tell us how the Jews ought to respond, but they fail to answer the question why the Israelites were chosen and not others. One Midrashic view states that the seven Noahide laws apply to all humanity, but once the special relationship was formed between God and Israel at Sinai, the Jews became priests to the rest of the world. Their purpose is to ensure that the non-Jews know about God. This view as expressed by David Novak could leave one with the impression that there is a descending order of importance—God, Jewish people acting in a priestly role, and the rest of humanity.[9] Why Israel was chosen to be the founding community for the Jewish faith and consequently the Christian and Muslim faith is probably best left as a mystery.

Alongside this particular bond for Israel, in some texts there is also a concern for the sojourner and resident alien (Exod 23:9; Lev 19:33-34; Deut 23:8). While the Law is eased a little to give them some privileges, the sojourners and resident aliens are clearly denied full worshiping and social rights within the Israelite community. However, our study has demonstrated distinct differences in attitude to the foreigner (וכר) in both the book of Ruth and Isaiah 56–66. Ruth's acceptance within the community equates with a form of naturalization without the ceremony to say she is now a Judean. Isaiah 56–66 endorses foreigners as participants in the cult which includes particular blessings when they keep justice and righteousness, accept the covenant, and observe the Sabbath. These promises function in the same way that circumcision functions in the Pentateuch and other texts, that is, there are criteria set for inclusion within the community. Levenson agrees that the participation of foreigners is developed even further with the statement in Isaiah

[8] R. R. Ruether and H. J. Ruether, *The Wrath of Jonah*, 245.
[9] D. Novak, *The Image of the Non-Jew in Judaism*, 53, 258, 412–13.

66 in which the foreigners can become priests.[10] Isaiah 56–66 challenges the basis of Israel's particularism by the claim that foreigners are in right relationship with God and therefore ought to be included within the worshiping community.

The pinnacle of the inclusive voices in the Hebrew Scriptures, then, is found in Isaiah 56–66 and the book of Ruth. In each of these books the foreigner becomes fully included within the life of the community. Along with the inclusion of the foreigner, there are quite clear expectations of the person. This could be perceived by some people as an exclusive action, and indeed in some ways it is.

We want to separate the acts of God from the response by humanity, beginning with the theological understanding that the grace of God is offered to all people as part of God's creation. However, when people choose to respond to this act of grace, we have to recognize that each community has its own set of requirements.[11] As Ruether says, "The ethics of mutual solidarity does not mean an anonymous universalism."[12] We need to explore how mutual solidarity can be maintained without sliding into factionalism on one hand, and an anonymous universalism on the other hand. It is quite apparent that there are both exclusive and inclusive voices in the biblical material; it is also clear that, in the case of inclusive voices, there will be certain obligations on the people who have joined with the Israelite community. In the Isaiah material no mention is made of circumcision. Instead there is the need to observe the Sabbath and keep the covenant.

As we have argued, Isaiah 56–66 and the book of Ruth stand out from other passages in the explicit manner in which they portray the inclusion of foreigners in the Israelite community. In both cases foreigners (נכר) are able to belong to the community.

---

[10] Levenson, "The Universal Horizon of Biblical Particularism," 163.

[11] Levenson, "The Universal Horizon of Biblical Particularism." We have to maintain the difference between the God centered understanding of God as creator and the availability of grace to every human person. As a response, the sub-groups will live under this grace, each with their own interpretations and responses to the one God, 168.

[12] R. R. Ruether and H. J. Ruether, *The Wrath of Jonah*, 245.

In Isaiah 56–66 foreigners are able to participate fully in the worship life of the community. They offer sacrifices in the house of prayer, minister to the Lord, love the Lord, and become the servants of the Lord. These roles in the past were usually designated to the Israelites alone. Trito-Isaiah confronts the Israelites to rethink their attitude to God and redefined the community to whom God will relate. The exclusion order in Ezekiel 44 confirms that the foreigners were assisting in the temple service at the time, or had been in the near past. If, as we suggest the final chapter of Isaiah is the pinnacle of the theology as presented in the prologue (Isa 56:1-8), then we have the exceptional proclamation that priests may be chosen from people of other nations.

Ruth accepts the faith of her mother-in-law and swears an oath in the name of Yʜᴡʜ. She becomes the savior of Naomi and ancestor of David, thereby forever becoming part of the Jewish nation.

Other passages demonstrate that some people believed God was able and willing to offer salvation to foreigners. Nineveh may not have been the focus for the book of Jonah, but the fact that this foreign town, which was anathema to Israel, was used is a significant indication of the depth of God's compassion to those other than Israel. The suggestion that the foreigners in 1 Kings 8:44-47 were heard and that their prayers would be answered is very unusual. All these voices tell us something about how foreigners were accepted by God and the Israelite community. Other passages in Isaiah (Isaiah 19, 25) tell us about aspects of an universalism which is different from the nationalistic proclamation of Isaiah 40–55 (chapter 3).

The theology in Isaiah 56–66 is the most explicit portrayal we have of foreigners' involvement in the worshiping life of the community. We are left in no doubt what the issues are for the writer of this material. Claims are made which counter the authority of the Torah and at the same time state quite categorically that these foreigners are able to participate in the same way as the Israelites. When we read the cry of the foreigner and the claims they make, in contrast with the exclusive voices of Ezra/Nehemiah and Ezekiel, it is easy to see how there might be groups with different attitudes vying to become dominant in the society of the time. We know from history (1 and 2 Maccabees) that the exclusive policies of Ezra/Nehemiah became the dominant theology until the time of Christ. In spite of this hardening of an exclusive attitude to foreigners within the Hebrew Scriptures, the inclusive messages of the above texts remained within these writings.

The natural tendency when people go to the Bible to find some ethical answer to a modern dilemma is either to study the Old Testament Law or to find the "words of Jesus" and apply them as law to the situation. For instance, in the case of divorce and remarriage, only texts which mention explicitly these issues would be quoted, no matter what their particular context or cultural situation. Very little reference used to be made to other stories that spoke of the love and forgiveness of God and the possibilities of new life in Christ. Reference to an overall picture of the ways of God is rare. Scripture is used as an authority for present day without recognition that the situation and culture are different, or that a new revelation of God might offer new insights. The story of Peter in Acts 10 illustrates how a new revelation of God can run counter to what has been the law for a certain community. In Acts 10, Peter experiences a vision which tells him he can eat unclean foods, in spite of the commands in the Torah that stated otherwise. His authority became the revealed vision rather than holy Scripture.

In his article "The Gap between Law and Ethics in the Bible," G. J. Wenham suggests that we have misinterpreted stories in the Old Testament because of our failure to understand the ethical principle that governed people's lives at the time. Furthermore, he suggests that this ethical stance is not always the same as the Law and indeed "ethics is much more than keeping the law."[13] In "biblical terms righteousness involves more than living by the decalogue and the other laws in the Pentateuch."[14]

The quote above is precisely the way in which the writer of Isaiah 56–66 justifies his position. It is clear from other texts in

---

[13] G. J. Wenham, "The Gap between Law and Ethics in the Bible," 17–29.
[14] Ibid., 19.

the Hebrew Scriptures that foreigners are no longer allowed to serve in the Temple (Ezekiel 44) and they have to separate from their foreign wives and children (Ezra/Nehemiah). Ezekiel, Ezra, and Nehemiah could call on the Law as it is found in the Torah (Genesis–Deuteronomy) to justify their actions of apartheid. The writer of Isaiah 56–66 had to call on an ethic of righteousness and faithfulness to make a claim for these people to remain within the community. Thus, although the Law might have condemned them, if people lived instead under the righteousness of God and followed that principle, then foreigners and eunuchs were to be treated in the same way as Israelites in the community.

We believe that the Bible goes beyond legal sanctions and is based on God's concern of an all embracing ethic in which life is sacred and God wants the best for all creatures. God is a relational being and wants people to be in covenant relationship with people. To live by righteous principles demands much more than if one lives by law. It is harder to determine in many instances what is the right action. We know the stories of Jesus in which he broke the Law because it was right to heal or to satisfy hunger on a Sabbath.

In the early Church Matthew struggled to gain authority for the inclusion of foreigners and their acceptance within the Christian community. How could he make this claim when he could not call on the Hebrew Scriptures to support his position? Indeed, the Hebrew Scriptures explicitly denied the inclusion of Gentiles.

Matthew draws on stories that people within the Jewish Christian community would know and uses them to give an alternative understanding. For example, four women from the Hebrew Scriptures are included in Matthew's genealogy of Christ—Tamar, Rahab, Ruth, and Bathsheba. Foreign women (some of whom were betrayed as sinners) are now perceived as acceptable because of their role in Jewish history, enabling the community to accept the idea that foreigners were included in the kingdom and proclamation of Jesus Christ. The stories give authority because they are present in the Hebrew Scriptures. However, we must note that Matthew's proclamation cannot be underpinned with the "authority" of any legal code. This was also the case for the writer of Isaiah 56–66.

Arising from this exploration of inclusive voices, the contemporary Church is faced with a number of challenges. How do we use Scripture to support new possibilities of inclusivity in the Church? Matthew was able to use his traditions to enable the new Jewish Christians to accept that Gentiles were welcome in their community. He called on an ethical base for giving authority to his proclamation by using stories from the Hebrew Scriptures rather than the Mosaic Law. The general lack of knowledge about the Bible today is a disadvantage in adopting Matthew's method. Trito-Isaiah used an "oxymoron" literary principle, based on righteousness and justice, to challenge those who wanted to exclude foreigners from the community. We face the challenge in the same way as Trito-Isaiah, who had to fight against those who quoted the Law as a basis for their position. However, we have to contend not only with Law in the Hebrew Scriptures as a basis for rejection but also the use of the words of Jesus to exclude certain people. This study of "inclusive voices" suggests that the alternative to such legalism is to turn to an *ethic based on righteousness, justice and love, which calls on stories and parables rather than the Law.*

In conclusion, we stand in a long line with those who have struggled with diverse voices in Scripture and how to proclaim a new message in opposition to the orthodox position. We can learn from the past how other writers have been inspired to proclaim their message, but we have to hear God's word for us in our time and trust that God wants to be in relationship with all people.

Bibliography

Aalders, G. C. *The Problem of the Book of Jonah.* London: Tyndale Press, 1948.

Achtemeier, E. *The Community and Message of Isaiah 56–66.* Minneapolis: Augsburg, 1982.

Ackroyd, P. R. *Exile and Restoration.* London: SCM Press, 1968.

_____. "An Interpretation of the Babylonian Exile: A Study of 2 Kings 20, Isaiah 38–39." *SJT* (27, 1974) 329–52.

Aejmelaeus, A. "Der Prophet als Klageliedsänger Zur Funktion des Psalms Jes 63:7–64:11 in Tritojesaja." *ZAW* (107, 1995) 31–50.

Ahlström, G. W. *The History of Ancient Palestine from the Palaeolithic Period to Alexander's Conquest.* Ed. Diana Edelman. Sheffield: Sheffield Academic Press, 1993.

Allen, L. C. *The Books of Joel, Obadiah, Jonah and Micah.* London: Hodder and Stoughton, 1976.

Anderson, R. A. *Daniel: Signs and Wonders.* ITC. Grand Rapids, Mich.: Wm. Eerdmans, 1984.

Bal, M. "Heroism and Proper Names, Or the Fruits of Analogy." *A Feminist Companion to Ruth.* Ed. A. Brenner, 42–69. Sheffield: Sheffield Academic Press, 1993.

Barker, M. *The Older Testament: The Survival of Themes from the Ancient Royal Cult in Sectarian Judaism and Early Christianity.* London: SPCK, 1987.

Bastiaens, J., Wim. Beuken, and F. Postma. *Trito-Isaiah. An exhaustive Concordance of Isa 56–66, especially with reference to Deutero-Isaiah. An example of computer assisted research.* Amsterdam: VU Uitgeverij/Free University Press, 1984.

Baumgartner, W., and L. Koehler, *The Hebrew and Aramaic Lexicon of the Old Testament.* Vol. I. Leiden: E. J. Brill, 1994.

Becking, B. "Continuity and Community in the Book of Ezra." *The Crisis of Israelite Religion: Transformation of Religious Tradition in Exilic and Post-Exilic Times.* Leiden: E. J. Brill, 1999.

Bedford, R. P. "On Models and Texts: A Response to Blenkinsopp and Petersen." *Second Temple Studies 1. Persian Period.* Ed. P. R. Davies, 154–63. Sheffield: JSOT Press, 1991.

Beentjes, P. C. "Inverted Quotations in the Bible: A Neglected Stylistic Pattern." *Bibl* (63, 1982) 506–23.

Begg, C. T. "The Absence of YHWH seba'ot in Isaiah 56–66." *BN* (44, 1988) 7–14.

Beuken, W.A.M. "Isa 56:9–57:13: An Example of the Isaianic Legacy of Trito-Isaiah." *Tradition and Re-interpretation in Jewish and Early Christian Literature,* 48–64. Leiden: E. J. Brill, 1986.

————. "The Main Themes of Trito-Isaiah." *JSOT* (47, 1990) 67–87.

Biggs, C. R. "Exegesis in the Book of Ezekiel. A Study of the Development of earlier Biblical material in the sermonic passages in the book." Ph.D. diss., University of London, 1975.

————. "The Role of the *nasi* in the Programme for the Restoration in Ezek 40–48." A paper presented to the Adelaide Theological Circle, 1988, in possession of C. R. Biggs.

————. "The Role of the Temple in the Book of Ezekiel." A paper presented to the Adelaide Theological Circle, 1989, in possession of C. R. Biggs.

Blank, S. *Prophetic Faith in Israel.* New York: Harper Bros., 1958.

Blenkinsopp, J. "A Jewish Sect of the Persian Period." *CBQ* (52, 1990) 5–20.

————. *Ezra-Nehemiah.* OTL. London: SCM Press, 1988.

————. "Second Isaiah—Prophet of Universalism." *JSOT* (41, 1988) 83–103.

————. "Temple and Society in Achaemenid Judah." *Second Temple Studies 1. Persian Period.* Ed. P. R. Davies, 22–54. Sheffield: JSOT Press, 1991.

Botterweck, G. J. and H. Ringgren, eds. *Theological Dictionary of the Old Testament.* Vol. 11. Trans. J. T. Willis. Grand Rapids, Mich.: Wm. Eerdmans, 1975.

Bronner, L. L. "A Thematic Approach to Ruth in Rabbinic Literature." *A Feminist Companion to Ruth.* Ed. A. Brenner, 146–69. Sheffield: Sheffield Academic Press, 1993.

Brown, F., S. R. Driver, and C. A. Briggs. *The New Brown-Driver-Briggs-Gesenius Hebrew—English Lexicon.* Peabody, Mass.: Hendrickson, 1979.

Burrows, M. *The Dead Sea Scrolls of St. Mark's Monastery, I. The Isaiah Manuscript and the Habakkuk Commentary.* New Haven: The American Schools of Oriental Research, 1950.

————. "The Literary Genre in the Book of Jonah." *Translating and Understanding the Old Testament: Essays in Honour of Herbert Gordon May.* Eds. H. T. Frank and W. I. Reed. Nashville: Abingdon Press, 1970.

Bush, F. W. *Ruth Esther.* WBC. Dallas: Word Books, 1996.

Campbell, E. F. *Ruth: A New Translation with Introduction, Notes, and Commentary.* AB. New York: Doubleday & Co, 1975.

Carr, D. "Reaching for Unity in Isaiah." *JSOT* (57, 1993) 61–80.

Carroll, R. P. *When Prophecy Failed: Reactions and Responses to Failure in the Old Testament Prophetic Traditions.* London: SCM Press, 1979.

Chilton, B. D. *The Isaiah Targum, Introduction, Translation, Apparatus and Notes.* The Aramaic Bible, Vol. 11. Edinburgh: T & T Clark, 1987.

Clements, R. E. *Isaiah 1–39.* NCB. London: Marshall, Morgan and Scott, 1980.

_____. "The Purpose of the Book of Jonah," *Congress Volume Edinburgh 1974.* Eds. J. A. Emerton et al. VTSuppl. 28. Leiden: Brill, 1975.

Clines, D.J.A. *Ezra, Nehemiah, Esther.* NCB. London: Marshall, Morgan and Scott, 1984.

_____. *The Dictionary of Classical Hebrew.* Sheffield: Sheffield Academic Press, 1993.

Conrad, E. W. *Reading Isaiah.* Minneapolis: Fortress Press, 1991.

Cross, F. L., E. A. Livingstone, eds. *The Oxford Dictionary of the Christian Church.* London: Oxford University Press (2nd ed.), 1974.

Cross, F. M. Jr. "The Themes of the Book of Kings and the Structure of the Deuteronomistic History." *Canaanite Myth and Hebrew Epic,* 274–89. Cambridge, Mass.: Harvard University Press, 1973.

Davies, G. I. "The Destiny of the Nations in the Book of Isaiah." *The Book of Isaiah.* Ed. J. Vermeylen, 93–120. Leuven: University Press, 1989.

Delitzsch, F. *Biblical Commentary on the Prophecies of Isaiah.* Trans. J. Martin. Edinburgh: T & T Clark, 1890.

Dell, K. "The Misuse of Forms in Amos." *VT* (45, 1995) 45–61.

De Vaux, R. *Ancient Israel: Its Life and Institutions.* Trans. J. McHugh. London: Darton, Longman & Todd, 1961.

DeVries, S. J. *1 Kings.* WBC. Waco, Tex.: Word Books, 1985.

Donner, H. "Jesaja LVI 1–7: Ein Abrogationsfall Innerhalb des Kanons— Implikationen und Konsequenzen." *Congress Volume: Salamanca 1983 VTSuppl.36.* Ed. J. A. Emerton, 81–95. Leiden: E. J. Brill, 1985.

Dyck, J. E. "The Ideology of Identity in Chronicles." *Ethnicity and the Bible.* Leiden: E. J. Brill, 1996.

Eissfeldt, O. *The Old Testament.* Trans. P. R. Ackroyd. Oxford: Basil Blackwell, 1966.

Elliger, K. "Der Prophet Tritojesaja." *ZAW* (49, 1931) 112–40.

Elliger, K., and W. Rudolph. *Biblía Hebraica Stuttgarten* 51a. Stuttgart: Deutsche Bibelgesellschaft, 1967/77.

Emmerson, G. *Isaiah 56–66.* OTG. Sheffield: JSOT Press, 1991.

Eskenazi, T. C. "Current Perspectives on Ezra-Nehemiah and the Persian Period." *CR:BS* (1, 1993) 59–86.

Fewell, D. N., and D. M. Gunn. *Compromising Redemption: Relating Characters in The Book of Ruth.* Literary Currents in Biblical Interpretation. Louisville: Westminster/John Knox, 1990.

Fischer, I. "The Book of Ruth: A 'Feminist' Commentary to the Torah?" *Ruth and Esther: A Feminist Companion to the Bible.* Ed. Athalya Brenner, 24–49. Sheffield: Sheffield Academic Press, 1999.

Fohrer, G. *Introduction to the Old Testament.* Trans. D. E. Green. London: SPCK, 1970.

Freedman, D. N., ed. *The Anchor Bible Dictionary.* New York: Doubleday & Co., 1992.

Fretheim, T. E. *The Message of Jonah: A Theological Commentary.* Minneapolis: Augsburg Publishing House, 1977.

Gelston, A. "Universalism in Second Isaiah," *JTS* (43, 1992) 377–98.

Gevaryahu, H. "The Universalism of the Book of Jonah." *Dor Le Dor* (10, 1981) 20–27.

Gottwald, N. K. *All the Kingdoms of the Earth.* New York: Harper and Row, 1964.

_____. *The Hebrew Bible: A Socio-Literary Introduction.* Philadelphia: Fortress Press, 1985.

Goulder, M. "Ruth: A Homily on Deuteronomy 22–25?" *Of Prophets' Visions and the Wisdom of Sages: Essays in Honour of R. Norman Whybray on His Seventieth Birthday.* Eds. Heather A. Mckay and David J. A. Clines, 307–19. JSOTSuppl.162. Sheffield: Sheffield Academic Press, 1993.

Gow, M. D. *The Book of Ruth: Its Structure, Theme and Purpose.* Leicester: Apollos, 1992.

Grabbe, L. L. *Ezra-Nehemiah.* London: Routledge, 1998.

Gray, J. *I & II Kings.* OTL. London: SCM Press, 1964.

Gunn, D. M., and D. N. Fewell. *Narrative in the Hebrew Bible.* Oxford: Oxford University Press, 1993.

Hals, R. M. *The Theology of the Book of Ruth.* Philadelphia: Fortress Press, 1969.

Hanson, P. D. "Israelite Religion in the Early Postexilic Period." *Ancient Israelite Religion: Essays in Honour of Frank Moore Cross.* Eds. P. D. Miller (Jr.), P. D. Hanson, S. D. McBride, 485–508. Philadelphia: Fortress Press, 1987.

_____. *The Dawn of Apocalyptic*. Philadelphia: Fortress Press (2nd ed.), 1979.

Hastings, J. *Encyclopaedia of Religion and Ethics*. Vol. 12, Edinburgh: T & T Clark, 1921.

Hayes, J. H., and J. M. Miller. *Israelite and Judaean History*. OTL. London: SCM Press, 1977.

Herbert, A. S. "Ruth," *Peake's Commentary on the Bible*. Ed. M. Black and H. H. Rowley. London: Thomas Nelson & Son, 1962.

Hillers, D. R. *Micah*. Hermeneia. Philadelphia: Fortress Press, 1984.

Hollenberg, D. A. "Nationalism and 'The Nations' in Isaiah XL–LV." *VT* (19, 1969) 23–36.

Hubbard, R. L. *The Book of Ruth*. NICOT. Grand Rapids, Mich.: Wm. Eerdmans, 1988.

Jones, D. R. *Isaiah 56–66 and Joel*. London: SCM Press, 1964.

Kaiser, O. *Isaiah 1–12*. 2nd Ed. London: SCM Press, 1983.

_____. *Isaiah 13–39*. London: SCM Press, 1974.

Klein, R. W. "The Books of Ezra and Nehemiah." *NIB* 3. Nashville: Abingdon Press, 1999.

Knight, G.A.F. *The New Israel: A Commentary on the Book of Isaiah 56–66*. ITC. Grand Rapids, Mich.: Wm. Eerdmans, 1985.

_____. *Ruth and Jonah*. London: Torch Bible Commentary, 1950.

Koch, K. "Ezra and the Origins of Judaism." *JSS* (20, 1974) 173–97.

Koenen, K. "Textkritische Anmerkungen zu schwierigen Stellen im Tritojesajabuch." *Bibl* (69, 1988) 564–73.

_____. *Ethik und Eschatologie im Tritojesajabuch. Eine literarkritische und redaktionsgeschichtlich Studie*. Neukirchener-Vluyn: Neukirchener Verlag, 1990.

Komlash, Y. "The Prophecy of Salvation." *Annual of Bar-Ilan University* (11, Bar-Ilan, 1973) 11–17.

Kraus, H. J. "Das Evangelium der unbekannten Propheten 40–66." *Kleine Biblische Bibliothek*, 235–55. Verlag: Neukirchener, 1990.

LaCocque, A., and P.-E. LaCocque. *Jonah: a Psycho-religious Approach to the Prophet*. Columbia: University of South Carolina Press, 1990.

Larkin, K.J.A. *Ruth and Esther*. OTG. Sheffield: Sheffield Academic Press, 1996.

Levenson, J. D. "The Universal Horizon of Biblical Particularism." *Ethnicity and the Bible*. Ed. Mark Brett, 143–69. Leiden: E. J. Brill, 1996.

Limburg, J. *Jonah*. OTL. London: SCM Press, 1993.

Linafeldt, T. *Ruth*. Berit Olam Series. Collegeville: The Liturgical Press, 1999.

Long, B. O. *I Kings with an Introduction to Historical Literature.* FOTL. Grand Rapids, Mich.: Wm. Eerdmans, 1984.

McCullough, W. S. "A Re-examination of Isaiah 56–66." *JBL* (67, 1948) 27–36.

McKay, H. "From Evidence to Edifice: Four Fallacies about the Sabbath." *Text as Pretext.* Ed. R. P. Carroll, 179–99. Sheffield: JSOT Press, 1992.

McKay, J. L. *God's Just Demands in Jonah, Micah, Nahum.* Fearn, Ross-shire, Scotland: Christian Focus Pubs., 1998.

McKenzie, J. L. *Second Isaiah.* Garden City, N.Y.: Doubleday & Co., 1968.

Magonet, J. *Form and Meaning: Studies in Literary Techniques in the Book of Jonah.* Sheffield: Almond Press, 1983.

Marcus, D. M. *From Balaam to Jonah: Anti-Prophetic Satire in the Hebrew Bible.* Atlanta: Scholars Press, 1995.

Martin, H. *A Commentary on Jonah.* Edinburgh: Banner of Truth Trust, 1978.

Miller, J. M., and J. H. Hayes. *A History of Ancient Israel and Judah.* London: SCM Press, 1986.

Moore, M. S. "Ruth the Moabite and the Blessing of Foreigners." *CBQ* (April, 1998) 213–17.

Morgenstern, J. "Isaiah 63:7-14." *HUCA* (23, 1950–51) 185–203.

_____. "Jerusalem—485 B.C.E.," *HUCA* (27, 1956) 101–79 (28, 1957) 15–47 (31, 1960) 1–29.

Mowinckel, S. *He That Cometh.* Trans. G. W. Anderson. Nashville: Abingdon Press, 1954.

Muilenburg, J. "Isaiah Chapters 40–66." *IB* 5, Nashville: Abingdon Press, 1956.

Myers, J. M. *Ezra-Nehemiah.* AB. Garden City, N.Y.: Doubleday & Co., 1965.

Neill, S., G. H. Anderson, J. Goodwin, eds. *Concise Dictionary of the Christian World Mission.* London: Lutterworth Press, 1970.

Neusner, J. *The Mother of the Messiah in Judaism.* Valley Forge, Pa.: Trinity Press, 1993.

Newsome, J. D. *By the Waters of Babylon.* Edinburgh: T & T Clark, 1979.

Nicholson, E. W. *Preaching to the Exiles: A Study of the Prose Tradition in the Book of Jeremiah.* Oxford: Basil Blackwell, 1970.

_____. "The Meaning of the Expression 'am haʾares' in the Old Testament." *JSS* (10, 1965) 59–69.

Nielsen, K. *Ruth.* OTL. London: SCM Press, 1997.

Noth, M. *Deuteronomistic History.* JSOT 15. Sheffield: University of Sheffield, 1981.

Novak, D. *The Image of the Non-Jew in Judaism.* New York: E. Mellen Press, 1983.

Odeberg, H. *Trito-Isaiah (Isaiah lvi–lxvi): A Literary and Linguistic Analysis.* Uppsala: Uppsala Universitets Arsskrift, 1931.

Odendaal, D. H. "The Eschatological Expectation of Isaiah 40–66 with Special Reference to Israel and the Nations," Ph.D. diss., Westminster Thelogical Seminary, 1966.

Orlinsky, H. M. "The So-Called 'Servant of the Lord' and 'Suffering Servant' in Second Isaiah." *Studies on the Second Part of the Book of Isaiah.* VTSuppl.14, 1–133. Leiden: E. J. Brill, 1977.

_____. "Nationalism-Universalism and Internationalism in Ancient Israel." *Translating and Understanding the Old Testament.* Eds. H. T. Frank and W. L. Reed, 206–37. Nashville: Abingdon, 1970.

Pauritsch, K. *Die Neue Gemeinde: Gott sammelt Ausgestossene und Arme (Jesaja 56–66).* AnBib 47, Rome: Biblical Institute Press, 1971.

Petersen, D. L. *Haggai and Zechariah 1–8.* OTL. London: SCM Press, 1984.

Polan, G. J. *In the Ways of Justice Toward Salvation: A Rhetorical Analysis of Isaiah 56–59.* New York: American University Studies, VII, vol. 13, 1986.

Rashkow, I. "Ruth: The Discourse of Power and the Power of Discourse." *A Feminist Companion to Ruth.* Ed. A. Brenner. Sheffield: Sheffield Academic Press, 1993.

Rendtorff, R. "The Composition of the Book of Isaiah." *Canon and Theology: Overtures to an Old Testament Theology.* Trans. M. Kohl, 146–69. Edinburgh: T & T Clark, 1994.

_____. "Isaiah 56:1 as a Key to the Formation of the Book of Isaiah." *Canon and Theology: Overtures to an Old Testament Theology.* Trans. M. Kohl, 181–89. Edinburgh: T & T Clark, 1994.

_____. *The Old Testament: An Introduction.* London: SCM Press, 1985.

_____. "Zur Komposition des Buches Jesaja." *VT* (34, 1984) 295–320.

Robertson Farmer, K. A. "The Book of Ruth." *NIB*, 11. 889–946. Nashville: Abingdon Press, 1998.

Robinson, G. "The Meaning of יד in Isaiah 56:5." *ZAW* (88, 1976) 282–84.

Rofé, A. "Isaiah 66:1-4: Judean Sects in the Persian Period as viewed by Trito-Isaiah." *Biblical and Related Studies Presented to Samuel Iwry.* Eds. A. Kort and S. Morschauer, 246–61. Winona Lake, Ind.: Eisenbrauns, 1985.

_____. "The Onset of Sects in Postexilic Judaism: Neglected Evidence from the Septuagint, Trito-Isaiah, Ben Sira, and Malachi."

The Social World of Formative Christianity and Judaism. Eds. J. Neusner, P. Borgen, E. S. Frerichs, R. Horsley, 39–49. Philadelphia: Fortress Press, 1988.

Rooy, H. F. "The Nations in Isaiah." *Studies in Isaiah.* Ed. W. van Wyk. Sydney: NSW Press, 1980.

Rowley, H. H. *Israel's Mission to the World.* London: SCM Press, 1939.

_____. *The Missionary Message of the Old Testament.* London: SCM Press, 1944.

_____. *The Servant of the Lord.* London: SCM Press, 1952.

Ruether, R. R., and H. J. Ruether. *The Wrath of Jonah: The Crisis of Religious Nationalism in the Israeli-Palestinian Conflict.* San Francisco: Harper & Row, 1989.

Salters, R. B. *Jonah & Lamentations.* OTG. Sheffield: JSOT Press, 1994.

Sasson, J. M. *Ruth: A New Translation with a Philological Commentary and a Formalist-Folklorist Interpretation,* 2nd ed. Sheffield: Sheffield Academic Press, 1989.

_____. *Jonah: A New Translation with Introduction, Commentary, and Interpretation.* AB. New York: Doubleday & Co., 1990.

Schramm, B. *The Opponents of Third Isaiah: Reconstructing the Cultic History of the Restoration.* Sheffield: Sheffield Academic Press, 1995.

Scott, R.B.Y. "The Book of Isaiah." *IB* 5. Nashville: Abingdon Press, 1956.

Scullion, J. J. "Studies in Isaiah cc. 56–66," Ph.D. diss., Theological Faculty, Institut Catholique, Paris, 1966.

Sehmsdorf, E. "Studien zur Redaktionsgeschichte von Jesaja 56–66." 1 and 11, *ZAW* (84, 1972) 517–76.

Seitz, C. R. "Isaiah 1–66: Making sense of the whole." *Reading and Preaching the Book of Isaiah.* Ed. C. R. Seitz, 105–26. Philadelphia: Fortress Press, 1988.

Sekine, S. *Die Tritojesajanische Sammlung (Jes 56–66) Redaktionsgeschichtlich Untersucht.* BZAW 175. Berlin: Walter de Gruyter, 1989.

Smart, J. D. *History and Theology in Second Isaiah. A Commentary on Isa 35; 40–66.* Philadelphia: Westminster, 1965.

Smith, D. *The Religion of the Landless: The Social Context of the Babylonian Exile.* Bloomington, Ind.: Meyer Stone Books, 1989.

Smith, P. A. *Rhetoric and Redaction in Trito-Isaiah: The Structure, Growth and Authorship of Isaiah 56–66.* Leiden: E. J. Brill, 1995.

Smith-Christopher, D. L. "The Mixed Marriage Crisis in Ezra 9–10 and Nehemiah 13: A Study of the Sociology of Post-Exilic Judaean Community." *Second Temple Studies 2. Temple and Community in the Persian Period.* Eds. T. C. Eskenazi and K. H. Richards, 243–65. Sheffield, JSOT Press, 1994.

_____. "Between Ezra and Isaiah: Exclusion, Transformation, and the Inclusion of the 'Foreigner' in Post-Exilic Biblical Theology." *Ethnicity and the Bible.* Leiden: E. J. Brill, 1996.

Snaith, N. H. "The First and Second Books of Kings," *IB* 3, New York: Nashville, 1954.

_____. "Isaiah 40–66. A Study of the Teaching of Second Isaiah and its Consequences." *Studies on the Second Part of the Book of Isaiah.* VTSuppl.14. H. M. Orlinsky and N. H. Snaith, 135–264. Leiden: E. J. Brill, 1967.

Steck, O. H. "Zu jungsten Untersuchungen von Jes 56:1-8, 63:7–66:24." *Studien zu Tritojesaja.* BZAW 203, 229–65. New York: Walter de Gruyter, 1991.

Stuart, D. *Hosea-Jonah.* WBC. Waco, Tex.: Word Books, 1987.

Sweeney, M. A. *Isaiah 1–4 and the Post-Exilic Understanding of the Isaianic Tradition.* BZAW 171. Berlin: Walter de Gruyter, 1988.

_____. "The Book of Isaiah in Recent Research." *CR:BS* (1, 1993) 141–62.

Talmon, S. "The Emergence of Jewish Sectarianism in the Early Second Temple Period." *Ancient Israelite Religion: Essays in Honour of Frank Moore Cross.* Eds. P. D. Miller, P. D. Hanson, and S. D. McBride, 587–616. Philadelphia: Fortress Press, 1987.

Thompson, J. A. *The Book of Jeremiah.* NICOT. Grand Rapids, Mich.: Wm. Eerdmans, 1980.

Throntveit, M. A. *Ezra-Nehemiah.* Interpretation. Louisville: John Knox Press, 1989.

Tollington, J. E. *Tradition and Innovation in Haggai and Zechariah 1–8.* Sheffield: JSOT Press, 1993.

Tomasino, A. J. "Isaiah 1:1–2:4 and 63–66, and the Composition of the Isaianic Corpus." *JSOT* (57, 1993) 81–98.

Towner, W. S. *Daniel.* Interpretation. Atlanta: John Knox Press, 1984.

VanGemeren, W. A., ed. *New International Dictionary of Old Testament Theology and Exegesis.* Vol. 1. Carlisle, Cumbria: Paternoster Press, 1996.

Van Winkle, D. W. "The Relationship of the Nations to Yahweh and to Israel in Isaiah 40–55." *VT* (35, 1985) 446–95.

Van Wolde, E. *Ruth and Naomi.* London: SCM Press, 1997.

Vawter, B. *Job and Jonah: Questioning the Hidden God.* New York: Paulist Press, 1983.

Vermeylen, J. "L'unitie du livve d'Isaïe" in *The Book of Isaiah.* Ed. J. Vermeylen, Louvain University Press, 1989.

Wainwright, G. "Universalism." *Dictionary of the Ecumenical Movement*, Eds. N. Lossky et al., Geneva: WCC Publications, 1991.

Watts, J.D.W. *Isaiah 1–33*, WBC. Waco, Tex.: Word Books, 1985.

_____. *Isaiah 34–66*. WBC. Waco, Tex.: Word Books, 1987.

Webster, E. C. "The Rhetoric of Isaiah 63–65," *JSOT* (47, 1990) 89–102.

_____. "A Rhetorical Study of Isaiah 66." *JSOT* (34, 1986) 93–108.

Weinberg, J. *The Citizen-Temple Community.* Sheffield: JSOT Press, 1992.

Wenham, G. J. "The Gap between Law and Ethics in the Bible." *Journal of Jewish Studies* (48:1, 1997) 17–29.

Westermann, C. *Prophetic Oracles of Salvation in the Old Testament.* Trans. K. Crim. Louisville: Westminster, 1987.

_____. *Isaiah 40–66.* Trans. D.M.G. Stalker. London: SCM Press, 1969.

Whybray, R. N. *The Second Isaiah.* OTG. Sheffield: JSOT Press, 1983.

_____. *Isaiah 40–66.* NCB. London: Marshall, Morgan & Scott, 1975.

Wildberger, H. *Isaiah 1–12.* Trans. T. H. Trapp. Minneapolis: Fortress Press, 1991.

Williamson, H.G.M. *Ezra and Nehemiah.* OTG. Sheffield: JSOT Press, 1987.

_____. *Ezra, Nehemiah.* WBC. Waco, Tex.: Word Books, 1985.

_____. "The Belief System of the Book of Nehemiah." *The Crisis of Israelite Religion: Transformation of Religious Tradition in Exilic and Post-Exilic Times.* Leiden: E. J. Brill, 1999.

_____. "Isaiah 63:7–64:11. Exilic Lament or Post-Exilic Protest." *ZAW* (102, 1990) 48–58.

Wilson, A. *The Nations in Deutero-Isaiah: A Study in Composition and Structure, Ancient Near Eastern Texts and Studies 1.* Lewiston, N.Y.: Edwin Mellen Press, 1986.

Wolff, Hans W. *Obadiah and Jonah: a Commentary.* Trans. Margaret Kohl. London: SPCK, 1986.

Zimmerli, W. "Prophetic Proclamation and Re-interpretation." *Tradition and Theology in the Old Testament.* Ed. D. Knight, 69–101. Philadelphia: Fortress Press, 1977.

_____. *Ezekiel 1.* Trans. R. E. Clements. Hermeneia. Philadelphia: Fortress Press, 1979.

_____. *Ezekiel 2.* Trans. J. D. Martin. Hermeneia. Philadelphia: Fortress Press, 1979.

_____. "Zur Sprache Tritojesaja," *Gottes Ofenbarung: Gesammelte Aufsätze zum Alten Testament,* 217–33. ThB 19, Munich: 1963.

Appendix

TABLE I

Proposals for the Redactional growth of Isaiah 56–66.

Author	Original Text	520–515 B.C.E.	440–420 B.C.E.	4th Century	3rd Century
Beuken		56:9–66:14	56:1-8; 66:15-22		
Kessler		56:9–66:15 = 515–475 B.C.E.	56:1-8; 66:16-24		
Pauritsch	587 B.C.E. 63:7–64:11	56:9-12; 57:1-13, 58-59, 60-62, 65; 66:1-4(6)	56:1-8; 57:14-19; 66:5(6,7)-16,(17); 66:18-23	66:24	57:20-21 no date; 63:1-6 = apocalyptic
Elliger	(538–519 B.C.E.) 63:7–64:11; 63:1-6	60–62; 57:14-19, Just after 515 = 56:1-2, 58; 59:1-20 Later but before 500 = 56:9–57:13; 65:1-7; 65:8-12; 66:1-4; 65:13-25; 66:5-17	Between 520 and Ezra 56:3-8; 66:18-22; 57:13c; 57:20-21; 58:13-14; 59:20		
Fohrer	63:7–64:11	66:1-4, 60, 61, 62	480 B.C.E.- 56:1-8; 56:9–57:13, 59, 450 B.C.E.- 57:14-21; 58:1-12; 58:13-14; 63:1-6	65	66:5-24

Author	Original Text	520–515 B.C.E.	440–420 B.C.E.	4th Century	3rd Century
Hanson	Early post-exilic 60–62; 57:14-21; 63:7–64:11; 58:1-12; 59:1-20; 65:1-25; 63:1-6	56:9–7:13; 66:1-16	475–425 B.C.E. redactional-framework 56:1-8; 58:13-14; 66:18-24		
Koenen	56:9-12; 63:7–64:11	57:14-19; 58:3-12; 59:1-15a; 60:1-18; 61:1-6 (7-9); 62:1-12; 65:16b-24; 66:7-14a	56:1, 2, 3-8, 11a; 57:1-13a, 17-18a; 58:1, 13, 15-20; 60:6b, 7, 9-10, 13-21; 61:10-11; 62:9ab; 63:1-6; 65:1-7, 8-15, 16a; 66:3, 5, 14b-17, 18-22		
Rendtorff Sweeney Carr Tomasino	These scholars have a redaction which includes all or part of Isa 56–66 as the final compilation of Isa 1–66		Rendtorff-56–66 Carr- 65–66 Sweeney-65–66, Tomasino-63–66		
Scullion		nucleus of 60–62 + lament either side 59 and 63–64 then 4 other strands[1]			
Sekine Redactor uses the texts of 8 different authors including Trito-Isaiah	63:7-10	Trito-Isaiah = 60–62; 57:14-19; 65:16b-23, 25; 66:7-16 Redactions 59:1-15a; 63:11b–64:3, 9-11; 64:4b-8; 66:1-4; 65:16b-23, 25; 66:7-16	56:1-5a; 56:9–57:13a; 58:3-14; 63:1-6; 65:2-16a; 66:5-6, 17, 18-24	Redactional parts; 56:5ab, 5bb, 6-8; 57:13b, 15bb, 18bb-19ab, 20f.; 58:1f.; 59:15b-21; 63:11a; 64:4a; 65:1, 24; 66:5f., 17, 18-24	

Author	Original Text	520–515 B.C.E.	440–420 B.C.E.	4th Century	3rd Century
Steck-Isa 56–66 never a separate book	40–55 + 60:1-9, 13-16; 61:1-11	60:10-11; 62:1-7	56:9–59:12, 15-21; 63:1-6	Post 301 63:7–64:11	300–270 56:1-8; 65:1–66:24
Vermeylen Pre-exile: 56:9-12; 57:6-13a; 57:14a, 17-19	Exile: 63:7–64:11; 65:16, 18b-20a, 21-22a, 23 + 66:7-14a 1st Redaction 57:15ab-16, 20; 60:22; 61:1-4, 7b-9; 62:4f.; 63:17; 64:2b-4a; 65:8-10, 24; 66:1f.	56:9–59:15a; 59:15b–62:5	58:1-3a, 5-12, 14b	57:5; 57:21; 59:5-8, 18b; 60:3-5, 7b, 11, 14-18, 21; 61:5-7a; 62:1, 6-9; 63:1-6; 65:1f., 6-7a, 11a, 12-15, 25, 63:3f., 5f., 14b, 17, 23f.	56:8; 60:4b, 9ab; 62:10-22; 66:20; 56:3-7; 66:18f., 21 Retouched in apoc. style; 59:12; 60:12, 19f.; 65:17-18a, 20b, 22b; 66:15f., 22
Westermann	Trito-Isaiah, Isa 60–62, 59, 63/64, 57:14-20; 65:16b-25; 66:6-16; 58:1-12?	56:9–57:13; 57:21; 59:2-8; 65:1-16a; 66:3f., 5, 17 = division between devout and sinful	60:12; 63:1-6; 66:6, 15-16, 20, 22-23 = modifies T-Is friendly attitude to foreigners	60:19f.; 65:17, 25; 66:20, 22f. = apocalyptic-alyptic. 4th strand = 56:1-2, 3-8; 58:13-14; 66:18-19, 21; 66:1-2	
Whybray	Exilic; 63:7–64:12	56:1-8, 57-62; 65:1–66:14	65:17, 25; 66:6, 15-23		

[1] J. J. Scullion, 'General Structure of Isaiah 56–66,' a John Scullion paper held in the United Faculty of Theology Library, Melbourne.

TABLE II

Connections within Isaiah 65.

Words, Phrases or Theological Concepts	References within Isaiah 65
those who fail to seek him, nation, people	vv. 1-5 connected through 1a, 1b, 2a and 3b
אלה (these) v. 5b	Gathers up the references to the people and named sins in vv. 1-5
YHWH is speaker	vv. 1-7, 12, 17-19
servants	vv. 8, 9, 13x3, 15
mountains	v. 7 and v. 9b
holy mountain	vv. 9 and 11, 25
descendants in v. 9	are the blessing in v. 8
my chosen	vv. 9, 15, 22
seek	v. 1 applies the verb to those who didn't seek YHWH. v. 10 is the converse
judgment on the apostate	vv. 2b-5 and 11-12
the imagery of call used negatively about the people, positively about God and the reconstituted community	vv. 1b, 12b, 24
because . . . therefore	the words connect v. 12b to v. 13a
but you	give an emphatic ring to the accusation which follows in vv. 11a, 12b
former troubles, former things	vv. 16b, 17a
I create	vv. 17, 18
be glad	vv. 18, 19
blessing	vv. 8, 16, 23
for behold, I create	v. 16b//17a + v. 18

TABLE III

Connections between Isaiah 66 and Isaiah 65.

Isaiah 66	Theological Link	Isaiah 65
66:3, 4	*people choose their own way*	65:1, 12b
66:3	*list of cultic sins*	65:3-7
66:4b	*a nation that did not call*	65:1, 12
66:5	*call to hear*	65:12
66:7-11	*the inheritance described in 66 is prophesied in 65:9*	65:8-9a
66:10	*the new Jerusalem*	65:18-19
66:12-14	*ideal conditions in Jerusalem*	65:19-25
66:14b	*the division between servants and enemies*	65:11-16
66:12-14	*the faithful are rewarded*	65:13-25
66:4, 6, 16, 24	*judgment*	65:7, 11-12, 13-16

TABLE IV

Texts relating to foreigners/eunuchs in Isaiah 56:1-8 that apply to Israelites in texts external to Isaiah 56–66.

Isaiah	Theological Concept	Texts external to Trito-Isaiah
56:2	*who keeps the Sabbath not profaning it*	Ezek 20:10-24; 22:8, 26; Neh 13:17ff.
56:3, 6	נכר	Gen 17, 12, 27; Exod 12:43; Lev 22:25; Ezek 44:9; 2 Sam 22:45, 46
56:3	*'shall surely separate me from his people'*	Ezra 9:1; 10:2, Neh 9:2; 10:28; 13:3
56:5	*I will give them an everlasting name which shall not be cut off eunuchs*	Deut 23:1 Lev 21:16-23
56:6	*to love the name of the Lord*	Deut 10:12; 19:9; 30:6, 16, 20, only the people of Israel are called to love the name of the Lord
56:6	*to minister to him*	Ezekiel, Chronicles, Num 18:1ff//56:6
56:7	*'to bring,' YHWH brings the Israelites out of Egypt*	Ezek 20:6, 35, 38
56:8	*to gather yet others*	Deut 30:3; 1 Sam 7:5; Ps 106:47; Isa 2:16; 11:12; Jer 40:2-12; 43:5; 54:7
56:6	*to be his servants*	Lev 25:55, other than Nebuchadnezzar only the Israelites have been named as the servants of God

TABLE V

Connections within Isaiah 56–66 as shown in the occurrence of words, phrases, and theological concepts.

No.	Word/Phrase/Literary Structure	Text References
1	*keeping the Sabbath holy*	Isa 56:2, 6; 58:13; 66:23
2	*ethical requirements and Sabbath command, 'profane'*	Isa 56:1-2
3	נכר	Isa 56:3, 6; 60:10; 61:5; 62:8
4	*to choose*	Isa 56:4; 65:12; 66:3-4
5	*'house' rather than 'temple'*	Isa 56:5, 7; 58:1, 7; 60:7; 63:7; 64:11; 66:1, 20
6	*my holy mountain*	Isa 56:7; 57:13, 15; 65:11, 25; 66:20; 65:2 as part of judgment oracle
7	*to gather yet others*	Isa 56:8; 60:4; 66:18. Implication of Isa 56:8 spelled out in 66:18-24
8	*cultic aberrations, apostasy*	Isa 65:3b-5, 7, 11; 66:3, 17; 64:11ff.; 57:5-9, 13; 58:3-14; 59:3-8, 13-15
9	*literary structure—65–66*	Isa 65:1-7 = judgment, 65:8-25 = salvation, 66:3-4 = judgment, 66:10-14 = salvation, 66:15-17 = judgment, 66:18-23 = salvation, 66:24 = judgment
10	*nations and tongues*	Isa 66:18
11	*'in them'—acts as a connecting link to identify the subject in 66:18-23*	'they shall come' (v. 18), 'among them' (v. 19), 'from them' (v. 19), 'they shall bring' (v. 20), and 'some of them' (v. 21)
12	*new heavens and new earth*	Isa 65:17 (development of 51:6; 42:5-9, 43:15-19); 66:22
13	*former things*	Isa 60–62; 65:17

No.	Word/Phrase/Literary Structure	Text References
14	*causal* כִּי	Isa 66:18 and 22 suggest link whereby vv. 22-23 build on pronouncement of vv. 18-21
15	*fire and judgment*	Isa 66:24; 66:6, 15-17 = within 66. Connections also to 59:15b-20; 63:1-6
16	*answer to prayer in 64:8-12* →	Isa 65:1
17	*'I was ready to be sought,'* *'when I called'*	Isa 58:9, 12; 62:2, 4, 12; 63:19; 64:4; 65:1, 10, 12b; 66:4
18	*'where is he' — 'here am I'*	Isa 52:6; 58:2, 9; 65:24. 65:1 answers the question 'where is he' from 63:11, 15
19	*a rebellious and stubborn people*	Isa 50:5; 63:9-10; 63:17; 64:5b; 65:1-2
20	*a similar view of the garden as negative*	Isa 57:3-10; 66:3, 17
21	*The identity of the servants*	Isa 56:6; 65:8, 9, 13x3, 15
22	*Links within and between 65:8-12 (but you did what was evil . . .) and vv. 13-16 (my servants shall . . .); 'therefore' (v. 13) response to 'because' (v. 12)*	Isa 65:8, 9b and vv. 11a, 12c; 65:13 response to 12b
23	*be glad and rejoice*	Isa 65:18-19; 61:7, 10; 62:2-5; 64:5; 65:12; 66:10, 14
24	*restoration of Zion*	Isa 65:22; 62:8
25	*trembles at my word*	Isa 66:1, 5; 64:2; 66:2
26	*use of the Hebrew* שׂמח	Isa 56:7; 66:5
27	*The theme of the people's own way versus God's way*	Isa 66:4; 56:11; 57:17; 58:13; 65:2
28	*connections between 65 and 66, particular themes = sacrificial sins, inability to listen, refusal to respond to Y*HWH*'s call*	Isa 66:3-4//65:11-12; 66:2, 5//65:24; 66:4//65:1, 6, 12; 66:10//65:18-19; 66:7-10 explains 65:8-9 and connects to 59
29	*hypocrisy condemned*	Isa 66:2b-3; 58:3-14; 59:3-8, 13-15; 65:3-5; 66:17
30	*you shall suck*	Isa 66:11, 60:16, also connects 66:11 to v. 12, 66:11-14 explains 65:9b-10; 66:14b//65:1-7, 11

No.	Word/Phrase/Literary Structure	Text References
31	*phrases common to 60–62*	Isa 66:12-14//60-62; 66:10-11//60:20, 61; 66:10//65:18-19
32	*judgment/salvation of oracles*	Isa 66:6, 15-16 (judgment) surround vv. 7-14; Isa 59:15b; 63:1-6 (judgment) surround 60–62
33	*his indignation*	Isa 66:14b; 57:8; 59:12; 62:11; 63:3, 11; 64:4; 65:23; 66:10
34	*sons and daughters from afar*	Isa 66:20; 60:4 (different agent of return)
35	*links between Isa 64 and 65*	Isa 65:5 verifies that God is indeed angry 64:5
36	*the promise of restoration*	Isa 65:22 has close connections with Isa 62:8
37	*before they call . . .*	Isa 65:24 connects with 65:1. Isa 58:9a
38	*The play on 'hear the word of the Lord'*	Isa 65:24; 66:2, 5 (positive references), Isa 65:1, 6, 12; 66:4 (negative)
39	*the birthing image of Zion*	Isa 66:7-10 explains 65:8-9, also connects with Isa 59
40	*structure of judgment oracles surrounding oracles of salvation*	Isa 66:6 and 15-16 surround the oracle vv. 7-14//Isa 15b-20 and 63:1-6 surround the salvation oracles of Isa 60–62
41	*called by a new name*	56:5; 62:2; 63:19; 65:15; 66:22

Author Index

Subject Index

Index of Biblical Texts

NEW TESTAMENT